NICOLE BROSSARD

ESSAYS ON HER WORKS

WRITERS SERIES 18
SERIES EDITORS:
ANTONIO D'ALFONSO AND JOSEPH PIVATO

Canada Council Conseil des Arts
for the Arts   du Canada

ONTARIO ARTS COUNCIL
CONSEIL DES ARTS DE L'ONTARIO

Guernica Editions Inc. acknowledges the support of
The Canada Council for the Arts.
Guernica Editions Inc. acknowledges the support of the Ontario Arts Council.

NICOLE BROSSARD

ESSAYS ON HER WORKS

EDITED BY LOUISE H. FORSYTH

GUERNICA

TORONTO – BUFFALO – CHICAGO – LANCASTER (U.K.)

2005

Louise Forsyth, Guest Editor
Guernica Editions Inc.
P.O. Box 117, Station P, Toronto (ON), Canada M5S 2S6
2250 Military Road, Tonawanda, N.Y. 14150-6000 U.S.A.

Distributors:
University of Toronto Press Distribution,
5201 Dufferin Street, Toronto, (ON), Canada M3H 5T8
Gazelle Book Services, White Cross Mills, High Town Lancaster LA1 1XS U.K.
Independent Publishers Group,
814 N. Franklin Street, Chicago, Il. 60610 U.S.A.

First edition.
Printed in Canada.

Legal Deposit — First Quarter
National Library of Canada
Library of Congress Catalog Card Number: 2005921430
Library and Archives Canada Cataloguing in Publication
Nicole Brossard : essays on her works / editor, Louise H. Forsyth.
(Writers series ; 18)
ISBN 1-55071-233-0
1. Brossard, Nicole. – Criticism and interpretation.
I. Forsyth, Louise II. Series: Writers series (Toronto, Ont.) ; 18.
PS8503.R7Z75   2005   C848'.5409
C2005-900852-0

Contents

Acknowledgments

My thanks go to Nicole Brossard for the extraordinary richness of her work and for the generosity with which she shares her vision, her passion, and her time. It has been a joy to work with her and her texts in the preparation of this volume. My thanks are extended as well to the contributors who received all my requests with good humour and whose appreciation of the brossardian *oeuvre* is wide-ranging, original, and — frankly — brilliant. Working in the combined symphony of the many voices heard in Brossard's texts, our voices here, and the many voices that have written elsewhere about her work — all of us celebrating in our own words the beauty Brossard has brought into each of our various lives — has made me feel, as never before, the rich potential of *connivance* among women: the real possibility of *re-inventing the world*. I want also to express my appreciation to Antonio D'Alfonso for inviting me to undertake this exciting project.

Acronyms

Works by Nicole Brossard

Referred to in the Essays

POETRY

AM	AMANTES[1]
AS	AUBE À LA SAISON
AV	AU PRÉSENT DES VEINES
CB	LE CENTRE BLANC (1970)
CR	CAHIER DE ROSES & DE CIVILISATION
DI	DOUBLE IMPRESSION
EB	L'ÉCHO BOUGE BEAU
GN	GREEN NIGHT OF LABYRINTH PARK
If	INSTALLATIONS (AVEC ET SANS PRONOMS)
Ie	INSTALLATIONS (WITH AND WITHOUT PRONOUNS)
L	LOVHERS
MC	MORDRE EN SA CHAIR
MJ	MÉCANIQUE JONGLEUSE
NV	LA NUIT VERTE DU PARC LABYRINTHE
P	LA PARTIE POUR LE TOUT
SL	SUITE LOGIQUE
TD	TYPHON DRU
VA	VERTIGE DE L'AVANT-SCÈNE

FICTION

A	L'AMÈR OU LE CHAPITRE EFFRITÉ (FICTION THÉORIQUE)
AB	A BOOK
BA	BAROQUE D'AUBE
BD	BAROQUE AT DAWN

Notes

1. Following all the essays contained in this volume, Works Cited contain only the works by authors other than Brossard. For references to Brossard's works, acronyms are given in parentheses immediately following citations. Full bibliographical information is given at the end of the volume in "Works by Nicole Brossard." Several of Brossard's works and translations of them have had more than one edition. Where this is the case, it has not been possible to provide page numbers for all editions.

Shadow, Soft *et soif*

NICOLE BROSSARD

en réalité l'espace s'amenuise
l'ardeur dessine ses noeuds de présence
ici et là en ville nous vivons
de convictions et de oui d'azur
nous avons le cheveu *dark*
et nos séductions sont comme des reprises
au fond d'un jardin. Observe bien les mots
ils vont bientôt   là
t'arracher au présent simple de l'abîme

*

à travers le feuillage des mots
quelques syllabes de nuit
regardons bouger
nos muscles de rêverie
les yeux devancés par la nostalgie
regardons
larmes, paumes et poings comme soif
et l'idée encore vague que vivre est
nécessairement un atout *inside language*

*

Shadow, Soft *et soif*

NICOLE BROSSARD

in reality space thins
ardor sketches its gnarled presence
about the city we live
on convictions yes and azure
our hair *sombre*
our seductions, reruns
at the garden's edge. Watch your words
they will soon   there
snatch you from the rift in the simple present

*

a few night syllables
through leafy words
let's watch
our dream muscles move
our eyes outstripped by nostalgia
let's watch
tears, palms and fists like thirst
the ever vague idea that living is
necessarily a plus *dans le langage*

*

être là toute une vie dans l'espèce flexible
avec ce réflexe qui persiste à vouloir
tout représenter de l'ivresse et des gestes
les morsures, les chambres avec leur creux
d'ombre et de souplesse, les fronts soucieux
notre fragilité
bien sûr que nous sommes sans réponse
à chaque baiser!

*

des idées de chute et de labyrinthe
comme si au bout de nos bras
tout ce qui existe était
fait pour un jour déplacer l'aube
lever le rideau sur le règne animal

alors je veille
parmi les canifs et la poussière

*

l'aube ne sombre pas
elle a ses majuscules
une élégante manière de juxtaposer
tout chauds les sourires
et blessures, si tu en veux

*

to be there a lifetime in the flexible species
with this reflex that keeps wanting
to depict everything about pleasure and gestures
bites, bedrooms with their shadowy, supple,
hollow spaces, knotted brows
our fragility
of course we go unanswered
with each kiss

*

ideas of falling and labyrinths
as if at arm's length
all that is was
made to shift dawn one day
reveal the animal reign

so I wake
in pocketknives and dust

*

dawn doesn't founder
with its capital letters
an elegant way of juxtaposing
smiles piping hot
and wounds if you'd like any

*

et si le tourment si ce qui anime
tes nuits de lecture et d'irréel
if dust on your fingers vibrate
adosse-toi à l'ombre
dans un endroit avec du bleu et du vide

il y aura c'est certain de l'eau dans tes yeux
et de la modernité et de la peur dans tes vêtements

*

tiens-toi bien dans le silence
à l'aube le verbe être court vite
dans les veines, corps céleste il file
comme après l'amour ou grain de sel
sur la langue le matin, goût d'immensité
il rapproche
de l'humidité première
viens m'embrasser
pense au grand pouvoir de l'eau
qui fait de nous un lieu[1]

and if torment if what quickens
your nights of reading and irreality
si la poussière vibre sur tes doigts
lean back on shadow
in a place with blue and emptiness

there will surely be water in your eyes
modernity and fear in your clothes

*

hold on in silence
at dawn the verb to be courses
in the veins, a heavenly body, it flies
as after love or grain of salt
on the tongue early morning, taste of immensity
it draws near
the first dampness
come kiss me
think of the great power of water
that makes a place of us

Notes

1. *Shadow Soft* et soif. 17, 18, 24, 26, 28, 31, 35. English translations of these poems, unpublished in French, are published here with permission.

In Conversation with Nicole Brossard

Louise H. Forsyth

I had the pleasure of spending a week in Nicole Brossard's home in February 2003, savouring the myriad pleasures of frequent encounters with her. Every day of my visit we sat down for a couple of hours to talk about her work, her writing, her travels, significant moments in her life as a writer, her views of the world in 2003. Our conversations took place in her dining room, across the transparency of the table's surface. We were surrounded by the works of art she has chosen for her personal space, and we were interrupted by the small events that punctuate and provide the rhythms of each day. Along with the regular flow of events, there were particularly exciting moments as well when copies of several of her new publications arrived, when friends gathered for dinner, when we strolled together in the streets of Montréal, and when the Conseil des Arts et des Lettres awarded Brossard the prestigious *Bourse de carrière*, with a citation written and read by Marie-Claire Blais, recognizing the exceptional contribution she has made to the vitality of Québec culture.

As I spoke with Brossard she was framed for my gaze in the breath-taking colours and forms of a large painting by Marcelle Ferron, a signator of *Refus global*. Such a context was profoundly appropriate for the words of this creative and revolutionary thinker. As the energy of other artists' visions and voices silently enveloped us, coming as well, for example, from the palimpsestic traces in works by Irene F. Whittome, I was carried away with Brossard's voice evoking visions of what might be in a world where women's *aerial letters* reached in and out to limitless horizons. These were special moments for me.

Instead of providing a transcription of this conversation in the form of an interview, I have asked Nicole Brossard to reflect upon the thoughts, ideas and passions she shared with me at that time. She has made the selection of topics most urgent for her today. What follows, then, is a number of fragments taken from a fascinating conversation. The words of the interview took us in many directions, followed many articulations, each with its own compelling logic, none of them in straight lines, and all of them exploring spaces of wonder, magic, and dazzling perspectives.

Fragments of a Conversation

Nicole Brossard

On vit dans une société fragmentée. On vit dans des fragments de récit. Et malgré tout, on recrée une cohérence.
[We live in a fragmented society. We live in story fragments. And in spite of all, we recreate a coherence.]

Nicole Brossard, 16 February 2003

Creativity

I like to think that the artist modifies the course of the intelligible and the emotional.[1] It may be a matter of objects, feelings, ideas, gestures or words. Artists show them to us from a new angle. Creation, as I see it, is a way of engendering sense where before there had been merely evidence of reality. The forms of creativity are numerous, but in a general way it can be said that they all revolve around sense. They exert their efforts in interrogating the world and reality, in thwarting censorship, in renewing ways of seeing, the value of words, of gestures, of images in order that we might better understand how what we invent reinvents the sense of our lives.

Writing

Writing is a way of tracing, of modifying, and of reinventing our presence in the world and in the face of the world. Presence in the face of the world which can also be associated with a desire to act on the world. "I write to make a statement of presence in language. In order for the *alive* to win out."[2] Writing is word to word, a slow plunge into an idea for staging the world. Writing can be done only in a body to body encounter with language, no doubt it involves listening as well, the emotion of making oneself available to one's inner voice. There are different ways of being in writing. I would say that writing brings into view landscapes, language structures that are infinitely attractive and mysteriously precise and that produce the desire to live, the desire both to be elsewhere and, paradoxically, to settle into the heart of the essential. Writing also secretes nostalgias, violences, lugubrious façades. It is living memory, incendiary memory. For my part, I have always made writing a place of pleasure, of quest, a space of dangerous intensity, a space for turbulence having its own dynamic.

In writing, everything is possible. Certainly, there is an end, but between *here* and *at the other end*, there is all that is needed, that is to say, material for dreaming. I favour personal transgression; that is to say I enjoy not conforming to what is expected of me. Playing with fire, with my freedom of expression, exploring – I have often said it, yes – I still write in order to explore and to understand. That is my primary motivation. My existence is a walk in writing; I don't take my eyes off the horizon. Recently I was trying to understand why the horizon, the sea, the desert were so important in my texts, and I said to myself that it is the distance which makes it possible for my looking to capture the world, to welcome it, to feel it desirable. And yet as much as I like to delve into a question, I distrust introspection. When I say that I like the horizon of writing, I'm also saying that I like to work its surface. Thus the surfaces of the genre become, in the geometrical sense of the term, *surfaces of sense*.[3]

Literature

Literature – space that is propitious for the imagination, for dreams, for interrogating the world – appears to me like a product filtered by history, sometimes censored, sometimes chosen, promoted, to make us know and think, to make us reflect and give pleasure. Literature requires time, to read it and to write it. It inserts itself into the time of the desired and the deferred. By nature it is a psychic reality from before the invention of computers, holography and virtual reality, which overturned our relation to time, to space, and to desire. Literature is not a matter of leisure; it is a matter of living in the place of the heart and of the gaze into a mystery which still persists. And especially, it keeps the *subject* in life and keeps it alive. Literature is a collective memory lodged in the heart of our intimacy and of the silence which generally accompanies reading.[4]

Poetry

For me poetry is limitless, radical and plural, flexible, trying, moving. Let's say that it hollows out shadows in the middle of the plexus, that it requires the taking up of the challenge of sense. It goes to the source of tradition and our old reflex to sing of love and death. I think that it will continue to traverse this century, like other centuries, just as much and as long as we know appetite, suffering or vital impulse. It will traverse the language, imprinting bites and burns upon it, like so many acts of presence, like a little light of hope. It will continue to offer its plays on words and on vertigo and to wrap itself around us like an identity, a memory. It will lead combats.

It is in poetry that I feel myself most happy. I find a space there, a sense of well-being in which my relation to the world is absolutely happy, living. A space where I feel myself integral, vigorous. No need for the mediation of characters in order to exist, just words, breath, a voice, energy arranging words, energy that makes a feast of life.

Le sens apparent [Surfaces of Sense]

This is a book-manifesto, of the kind with intentions of solidarity, a passionate book, quickened by love, revolt, the complexity of things. It is the first book of the cycle which includes: *Amantes* (Lovhers) , *Picture Theory, La lettre aérienne [The Aerial Letter], Sous la langue [Under Tongue]*. It is the book in which my fascination for the spiral appears for the first time like a fetish metaphor which was at the heart of my work for several years and which was replaced by the hologram. Obviously, "le sens apparent" is also an expression that reveals the need for questioning the *apparent sense* of reality. Writing is, by definition, the interrogation of sense. For a woman, the interrogation of the apparent sense of the organization of society leads her to question the meaning/ sense of her own life.

A Fetish Sentence

> *Une lesbienne qui ne réinvente pas le monde est une lesbienne en voie de disparition.*[5]
> [A lesbian who does not reinvent the world is a lesbian on the path to disappearance.]

For me the word *lesbian* is laden with an existential flavour and fervour that derive from our faculty for dreams, imagination, utopia.[5]

Reinventing the world is not only launching it again in a new landscape, but also activating this new landscape. This is a sentence which speaks to the constant need for creativity in those women whose difference is a source, all at the same time, of refusal and of pride – the need for creativity so that their existence, what makes sense in it, is not ignored.

This is something we know: nothing is ever

achieved definitively. Proof of this can be seen in the setbacks being recorded presently in the notion of democracy, indeed even that of humanity. Just think of the increasingly numerous intrusions that are being made into people's private lives. Feminists said *the personal is political*. Unfortunately, it now seems that political expediency has distorted this statement wiht the result that people's private lives can be invaded in the name of the fight against terrorism and for commercial ends.

I have always had a tendency to project onto the groups that I feel I belong to qualities that are important to me. Among these are creativity, invention, combat for change. And so, it is normal that I should project onto lesbians and onto women in general a knowledge, a desire for lucidity.

A whole generation of lesbian feminists saw in the word *lesbian* an equation with the words *autonomy, freedom, creativity, audacity, pleasure*. Lesbians appeared as bearers of a symbolic charge going well beyond a sexual practice. They assumed an avant-garde role in the combat being led against patriarchy and its structures of alienation and domination of women. As soon as the word *lesbian* is replaced by the word *homosexuelle [homosexual]*, it is easy to see that the two words are not invested with the same solidarity.

The lesbians and *urban radicals*, about whom I speak in *The Aerial Letter,* are feminists in a state of revolt, lucidity and utopia. The lesbian culture was, speaking culturally and literarily, an important lever in the feminist movement. Perhaps it is uniquely within that context that lesbian culture was able to flourish. There remains here and there pockets of lesbian culture, but on the whole lesbians seem to have become *gay*. They seem to me to have adopted a lifestyle much closer to the *gay* movement than to the lesbian movement.

The Feminine Body

For whoever looks, it is an irresistible, obsessing body. For whoever possesses it, it is a marked body. A woman in a woman's body is all that is most complicated, if you forget the body and you think only of her. The question is trying to know what having this body means to her in reality and in the fiction in others' heads. In my office I have stuck up on the wall a photo from a work by Joseph Kosuth where he shows a chair, a photo of a chair, and a poster on which there is the definition of the word *chair*. Reality, representation and the word-definition. Wholeness for a women is knowing that she is all of this when, with her entire body, she stretches out majestically toward life.

Characters

The characters of my novels are *pretexts* which permit

me to reflect, to install landscapes in which I can nego-
ciate with reality, interrogate the world. I clearly see
where my limits are insofar as interactivity between
characters is concerned. In any case, that is not my first
intention. My motivation is elsewhere, a good deal in
the writing, but also in the *mise en apparition [staging
the appearance],* so to speak, of life, of emotions, of
thoughts.

I have also noticed that in most of my novels I always
bring in five characters. Their roles and characteristics
can be broken down this way: one similar (Marielle in
French Kiss, Mélanie in *Mauve Desert*), two relational
alter egos (Angela Parkins in *Mauve Desert*, Carla
Carlson in *Hier*), one contrasting character having positive characteristics (Kathy Kerouac in *Mauve Desert*) and
an opposing figure (Longman in *Mauve Desert*).

I believe that the characters to whom I am most
attached are those of *Mauve Desert*. As well, it was that
attachment, that desire to know more about them
which was partially responsible for the novel's structure. As a result, through wanting to know the characters of Mélanie, Kathy Kerouac, Angela Parkins better,
it became necessary for me to invent with regard to
them, to weave relations among the women. This is
what led to the central part of the novel.

In fact, the characters I'm most happy with are the
ones whose portrait is incomplete, those who remain at
the stage of a sketch and who make it possible, in spite
of everything, to question life and create an environ-

ment propitious for emotion and the pleasure of the text. To put it briefly, characters interest me if they make it possible for me to question life.

There are as well the few masculine characters: Longman in *Mauve Desert*, Fabrice Lacoste or even Descartes in *Hier*, John in *Picture Theory*, others who here and there have secondary but symbolically charged roles, as in *Baroque at Dawn*. I don't think that characters who have nothing to do with the author can exist, unless they're simple passers-by.

Connivance

One part of my connivance with women showed up in activities linked in the first instance with literature or cultural life. It started with the film *Some American Feminists* with Luce Guilbeault; then there was the creation of the feminist newspaper *Les Têtes de pioche [Battle-axes]* and the collective work around the play *La nef des sorcières [A Clash of Symbols]*. Next there was the organization of the theatrical show *Célébrations* in collaboration with Jovette Marchessault and, of course, *L'anthologie de la poésie des femmes au Québec* with Lisette Girouard, of which we have just launched the second edition bringing in twelve new poets. As far as longer term work is concerned, there was *La théorie, un dimanche [Theory, One Sunday]*, a fine adventure of encounters, discussions, sharing, friendship and writing with Louky Bersianik, Louise Cotnoir, Louise Dupré,

Gail Scott and France Théoret. I work in places where there are affinities. That is, for me, the best way to respect the differences which appear in the course of working together. And then, I believe that I must also mention the importance of encounters with translators like Barbara Godard, Suzanne de Lotbinière-Harwood, Patricia Claxton, in the same way as university researchers, like you, for instance. Connivance and projects offer a good menu. Work spaces among women linked by a project are stimulating and productive, and I have always associated pleasure, friendship and festivity with them.

Men of Interest

Even if there are few masculine characters in my novels, it is clear that I engage in a dialogue with certain ones among them. Across the centuries, the cultures and the continents. Among my preferred companions: Leonardo da Vinci, Rainer Maria Rilke, Roland Barthes, Antonio Tabucchi. We forget too easily how marvellous it is to be able to choose the men and women of other centuries with whom we wish to pursue a conversation. Literature and books make it possible for us to converse with those with whom it seems to us we have things to share, to discuss.

The City, Montréal

The city, I associate it with movement, with spectacle, with circulation, and with the continual flux of destinies. But also with acceleration and with fragmentation. Everything goes quickly; you can know only some neighbourhoods, some faces. Each time you must reconstitute the coherence of the whole. If I think of the Montréal of my childhood, I think to the east and to the west, to the *downtown* [originally spoken in English] recounted by my father, who transformed the city centre of Montréal into a mythical place made up of pleasures, freedom, and spectacles. It is this Montréal which dwelt in me during all my childhood and my adolescence. But there was also the forbidden Montréal which was the one to the east of *la rue Saint-Laurent*, that is the French Montréal where the poor, the delinquents, the ordinary people lived. There are times when I walk in Montréal for pleasure, as if I were in a strange city. The city remains for me a place of creative *flânerie*. I have always thought that cities were like mythic jungles for writers; we clear a path for ourselves, we dream, we play around with an infinite number of small desires and simple joys.

There is a fascination for Montréal which typifies my Québec literary generation for whom urbanity, modernity and writing were associated with a space for freedom, transgression and avant-garde. It is interesting to note that in this sense anglophone poets of Montréal celebrated Montréal well before us. In my novel *French Kiss*, which has just been republished in Toronto with my first two novels under the title of *The Blue Books*, moving through Montréal became a metaphor for moving through language. Language work and displacement work, once again work of passage.

I dream that one day Montréal will become as mythic as other cities have become through the slant of literature: Buenos Aires with Borges, Dublin with Joyce, Trieste with Umberto Saba and Italo Svevo, Prague with Franz Kafka.

Travels, Being Elsewhere

Travelling makes me feel entirely like this moment of my existence is intense and right. I love the receptivity that is mine when I travel. It is a way of absorbing everything, an excessive presence to everything, which installs itself in us when we are in a period of creation. There are many cities in my novels: Buenos Aires, New York, London, Québec and Rimouski with the river. Like many, I am particularly happy and inspired when I am between two places; this means then that I love the plane and the train. These times of passage put me into a state of lucidity, of tension, of stimulation which causes me to throw myself into my writing notebooks. All states of passage inspire me, stimulate me, whether it is the passage from one language to another, a chemical process of transformation, or a change in someone's identity. All that stimulates my motivation for understanding, my faculty for dreaming, as if ideas, thoughts, life were shifting, had a goal, a hope.

It is certain that while travelling daily responsibilities disappear and there is a space of freedom that moves in. Journeys are undoubtedly linked as well to my desire for *horizon*, about which I spoke earlier. I need *space*. For me, it is having the space to move and to see far which brings the happiness of living. Vertical cities also have their horizon.

The Body, Humanity, the Spiritual

We who thought that feminism would help us reclaim our stolen humanity now find that we are entering into an era when science, neo-liberalism and globalization seem to be blurring the paths leading to an understanding of our humanity. Now that the multinationals of biotechnology have reached the point of manipulating and commercializing our genes and those of other *kingdoms*, what will happen to that supreme value called our humanity and which, until now, has theoretically served as a guarantee for us against systemic dehumanisation? We are giving our consent to drawing ever more close to a form of profanation of *the principle of humanity*, to borrow the title of Jean-Claude Guillebaud's book.[6] It is certain that the configuration of the word *humanity* has always changed. This is because cultures, the state of science and political wills have chosen to exclude whole groups from humanity, starting with women and slaves. What makes the value of a human being? Between the highest scientific performance and the bloodiest barbarity, will the principle of *humanity* manage for very much longer to produce anything other than illusion? These are questions that haunt me.

Silence

One enters a silence as one enters a space. One can make silence within oneself, but one can also enter into a silent room or a situation where silence is required. Silence is a punctuation. It is often there that emotion nests. I need silence; I need to create a void; in short, I need my *zen* moments in life and writing. Moments of extreme presence, of lucidity when I have the impression of working simultaneously on several levels: intellectual, spiritual, emotional, physical, light. Silence is an ally of concentration, of contemplation, of capture in each of our cells.

Silence, it is also presently a writing project.

The Present, Presence

I am a woman of the present; that is what I have always been, from *Le centre blanc* ["the white centre"] right up to *Hier*. And yet I find it difficult today when I realize that there is suddenly too much present, around us, as if we were doing nothing other than spanning across what is present and multiplying futile gestures. Present, speed, sensations are elements which have always seduced me. And yet I am unable to separate myself from the slowness that is so necessary for writing and for reading, for emotion and for desire. Therefore, in order to understand, I am trying to produce encounters between the present that I associate with silence and presence and the volatile present that short-circuits ancient odours secreted in the course of the last five centuries.

Notes

1. Translation of this conversation was done by LHF.
2. Nicole Brossard is quoting herself here, as translated by Susanne de Lotbinière-Harwood in *She Would Be the First Sentence of My Next Novel/ Elle serait la première phrase de mon prochain roman* 133.
3. Translator's note. During our conversation in French, Brossard used "un sens apparent" here: "apparent sense." This is the title of the prose work she published in 1980. Fiona Strachan translated this title as "surfaces of sense," a felicitous choice which I have retained here. See section below on *Le sens apparent.*
4. Translator's note. The word *littérature,* like *poésie* in the following section, is feminine in French. This gives the entire discussion about *literature* and *poetry* a feminine aura, as though enjoying literature and poetry meant entering a territory where women's presence and agency illuminate experience, since articles, pronouns and agreements of *nous* are all in the feminine. The English *it* does not begin to capture this flavour.
5. This sentence, with the magical powers Brossard attributes to it, appears in several places in her work.
6. Jean-Claude Guillebaud. *Le principe d'humanité.* Paris: Éditions du Seuil, 2001.

To Write: In the Feminine Is Heavy with Consequences

LOUISE H. FORSYTH

Les mots m'enflamment [Words inflame me (H 14)].

...to write in lesbian (Marlatt 118)

it's been a relief to write poetry, it's been just room
        to live (Brand 195)

help me write words/ in this night in this world (Pizarnik)

If you are reading the words on this page I hope that you have already read and savoured in the preceding pages Nicole Brossard's recent poems and her reflections on what matters and has mattered most to her as a writer.[1] Her words vibrate with the ardent and lucid voice of a wonderful artist. They offer invitations to try things out for ourselves in places we may have not yet explored. They call us to listen to the passionate sounds of our own silences. They are a gift and an appeal to renew the dawn. They echo the direct urgency that I hear in the voice of the Argentinian poet Alejandra Pizarnik: *help us write words in this night in this world*.

It has been my experience that the words in Brossard's texts unfold into passages of new discovery where I recognize things that I knew but have never before had words for. To paraphrase Dionne Brand, a writer for whom, like Brossard, writing is a matter of visceral necessity, and who, also like Brossard, has transformed Canada's socio-cultural landscape, "it's been a relief" for me to read her poetry and prose, "it's been just room to live."

Each essay in this volume addresses the centrality in Brossard's work of words and of writing. Each reveals the inflammatory and radical freshness of her approach to language in all its many functions. Each highlights the fact that Brossard's words have the potential to work with us in the re-invention of reality, knowledge, and ourselves. Each underscores, from many different perspectives, that writing *je suis une femme*, while joining with other passionate, conniving women to *écrire au féminin* is "heavy with conse-quences."

Brossard's works are always experimental. She does not ever allow readers of her texts to take her words for granted. There always seems to be some mysterious something else to be teased out. The quiet intervals, subtle echoes of sound, margins, breaks, tango-like alternating rhythms of ardent tensions and sensual hesitations can be more expressive than surface mean-ings. Her spare, carefully chosen or designed words make things happen; as Parker discusses in her essay, they are above all performative as they crisscross unpre-dictably on her white pages; they produce tears and rips in familiar patterns. Her punning and plays on words cause clear boundaries to fall away. This is by way of effective resistance to the performative linguistic formulae of hegemonic discourse that imposes norms regarding subjectivity and summons "us to do things with prescribed cultural messages" (see Parker). Silences and intensely dynamic white spaces that punctuate Brossard's words speak as enigmatically as the words themselves. The highly charged synergy passing among her words in arteries other than normal syntactic and narrative paths causes her texts to pulse with the rhythms of emotional, erotic, intellectual and spiritual ardour. Words are means to produce sharing among real writers and readers – along with textual and virtual ones – as they work together like creatively engaged translators to make meanings out of personal experiences and collective lives. As Hunter shows in her study of writing as articulation and re-articulation in Brossard's use of words, Brossard has adopted and sustained a writing project which is nothing less than a dynamic, experimental and creative process for the never-ending re-invention of the world and of life itself, making imaginative use of words – freed of their conventional, deadwood meanings and placements – in ever-renewed ways of speaking and writing:

> Lente émergence du désir dans l'inavouable de son projet de transformation de soi et de la collectivité. Inavouable volonté de changer la vie, de changer sa vie. [...] C'est alors que les mots se vident de leur sens ou encore qu'ils prennent un autre sens, une autre tournure dans les événements de la pensée. Les mots commencent à tourner sur eux-mêmes, incitant à la réflexion, incitant la pensée à de

nouvelles approches de la réalité. C'est alors aussi que les mots [...] vont devenir des stratèges indispensables pour affronter la réalité sur ses deux versants: celui du fictif et celui du réel (*LA* 44).

Desire slowly emanates from what is inadmissible in her project: transformation of the self, and the collectivity. Inadmissible will to change life, to change her life. [...] This is when words make themselves void of sense or take on another meaning; take a new turn in the sequence of thought's events. Words begin to turn round on themselves, inciting reflection, inciting thought toward new approaches to reality. And it is also when words [...] becom[e] indispensable strategies for confronting reality's two slopes: the actual and the fictive (*AL* 67-8).

As this quotation shows, and as Hunter discusses, the consequence of words used in such lucid ways is to provide a previously unexplored basis for women and men to site themselves on the social stage as moral agents. Conley argues convincingly in her essay that Brossard is seeking to incite the development of networks of "the intersecting trajectories of sensual, thinking women," all the better to nurture "the transformative possibilities of women's engagement with history and story" (McPherson).

What are some of the other heavy consequences that result when a woman writes and publishes the first person statement: "I am a woman" and then works to heed the desires of this speaking voice as they drive the mind and imagination in her sexed and gendered body, ardently aroused by the sensations of which she is newly aware? Into what spaces will her reflections take her? Brossard's works show that these consequences are endless and inexhaustible. The exploding spaces are astonishing. Cultural traditions have been largely silent about the experiences of women's bodies: sexuality, menstruation, giving birth, rape, violence, pleasures and fears. Brossard evokes these in all their unique specificity, and they achieve particular intensity in scenes of passionate *jouissance* when women loving and desiring other women transport themselves into new dimensions. She affirms and celebrates the realities of women's ardent presence by inventing characters and poetic voices who venture into the terrains of silence that have traditionally stifled women's breath. She proposes unexpected perspectives on women, whereby they either take shape and make sense or else reveal the intractable forces that keep them mute. Brossard has said that silence is one of her most urgent preoccupations today. In her essay, Campbell examines many of the complexities and contradictions surrounding the exploration of silence in Brossard's work, including the paradoxical tensions among silence, words, and meaning. Is it possible to experiment with silence in words? Brossard affirms the powerful significance of women speaking and writing in the cultures of the modern city, while at the same time her words produce awareness of the need for access to meaningful silences, far from the increasingly invasive noise of today's realities.

What Brossard's work shows is that it is not nearly enough to bring hidden and unspoken experiences to the surface where they might be represented using the tools of dominant cultures. The powers of patriarchy and oppression have penetrated much more deeply than surface representations in words and images. They have penetrated into minds, spirits and bodies in order to establish the very structures for thought, feeling, knowledge and memory, the structures that determine what makes sense, what has value, what seems real, what acts are conceivable and possible.

The consequences of writing "I am a woman" cause us to interrogate these structures and the meanings they impose. These consequences require that we *drift* into unexplored realms where our sense of ourselves, our past, our stories, and our experiences can come together in new configurations. Following Brossard in these explorations is an exciting aspect of reading her work, for they take us into dazzling virtual realities, always on the move, always reaching out to new horizons. Brossard rejects all world views determined by the principle of metaphor, built on hierarchy, authority, fixity, linearity. Working in her writing with principles of metonymy whereby fragments whirl together momentarily into unexpected configurations that give a glimpse of coherence and then move on, she chooses words that will take her readers and her characters into places where dynamic structures swirl. It is in such places that the neglected and unexplored shards of women's lives can shimmer toward sensual, intellectual and spiritual realization.

A striking consequence in Brossard's work of writing "I am a woman" has been the emergence of what Knutson calls in this volume "new tropic interpretive structures" in the form of the hologram, which captures so effectively the virtual structures where her words accomplish their explorations and where normative notions of depth and perspective are shattered. Holograms appear in the dazzling light of women's desire and passion, and then they disappear, all the better to appear again with some slight difference. Holograms also have the remarkable quality of having all of their information contained in each of their fragments. Are they real or just optical illusions? What is real? What are illusions? What is fiction? What is imagination or fantasy? The elusive forms of holograms give fleeting reflection, shape and context in Brossard's work to desire, writing, memory, and presence in the world. They fire readers' own desires to *delire* (see Holbrook in this volume). The essays of Conley and Knutson study holograms as models for consciousness, writing and memory in *Picture Theory* and throughout the electric circuits of her texts. I would add that she has been *drifting* on hologram-like tropic interpretive structures ever since *French Kiss*, and probably earlier, when the downtown of Montréal or any other modern city figured as an implicit hologram in whose networks the wired characters could effort-

lessly zip about or morph in both form and identity.
The trope of the hologram is a fundamental challenge
to all the presumptions of patriarchal ideologies. It
opens spaces and spheres for women's realities that
could not exist on other terms. Although never stable
or permanent it offers a vision of a luminous whole
that might give one's life sense in an incessantly changing universe.

We might ask ourselves whether such a radical shift
in perception is anything more than illusion. Yet
Brossard knows that modern science and information
technologies are revealing more and more cogently that
illusion may well lie on the side of the generally held
common-sense belief in material structures based on
three dimensions of space and one of time. It seems
that this belief is no more reliable than the rigid views
of those who forced Galileo to recant his knowledge
and that indeed the complex circuits of human thought
and memory may be more like mobile holograms producing virtual images than the fixed containers of
knowledge they are normally conceived to be (see
Bekenstein, "Are You a Hologram?").

And so the contributors to this volume show that
one discovers when reading Brossard's texts that the
heavy consequences of writing *I am a woman* produce
the necessity to re-think the very bases on which one
constructs one's sense of physical being in the material
world, one's sense of self, subjectivity and identity,
one's sense of moral agency, one's sense of relating to

others, and one's sense of knowledge and reality. Godard explores in her essay the ways in which Brossard was working her way through some of this radical re-thinking during the 1980s. Through Brossard's revolutionary simple words, nothing is left as it was in the world of dominant cultural institutions. Her words incessantly open passages into new ways of thinking and being, ways that resonate with the silences in many women's lives. Holbrook's exploration of the ramifications of *delire* through the many possibilities of creative translation provides an idea of how far one can go on the wings of Brossard's words.

Still, one cannot exist, one cannot even speak or write entirely outside hegemonic institutions and the traditions they perpetuate. Language, for all its problematic sexism and other biases, is at the core of all cultural traditions; words and images – that one can never thoroughly cleanse of the connotations they have acquired through repeated, normative usage – form the basis for all modes of communication in society. These sullied words are all we have to articulate and share what we know. Brossard's writing weaves in ludic gambols throughout patriarchal structures and their institutions. Her words use but also upset *common sense*, dominant discourse, and prevailing beliefs that order, classifications and authoratative assertions reflect transcendent realities. Very often she introduces devices of intertextuality and interdiscursivity in order to echo the voices of other radical thinkers of the past and present, men as well as women, whose words and ideas have taken them *outside the box* in illuminating ways, or else to parody the automated voices of official pronouncements. Conley discusses Brossard's particularly innovative approaches to intertextuality as she re-reads and re-casts words in others' texts. As Potvin suggests in her essay, Brossard *flirts* with institutional discourse, using it for her own exploratory and creative purposes, while revealing its vulnerability and flaws when its presumed logic and coherence go unexamined. As McPherson suggests, Brossard *flirts* for purposes of negotiation with norms of autobiography and referentiality in fiction as she explores, while also challenging, her own and other individuals' sense of coherent self and world. She also *flirts* with literary conventions, never hesitating to blur or cross the boundaries of genre. As Dupré and Godard discuss in this volume, Brossard's synthesis of the devices of poetry, fiction, autobiography, drama and theory has produced texts that resist generic classification and that are both astonishing in their beauty and astonishing in their non-canonical suggestive power.

In Brossard's works, words slip sensually and sensuously among their literal meanings; they evoke apparently anomalous connotative associations; they draw attention to their own literal materiality in sound and substance, and they play with themselves in halting or breaching structures of syntax and narration. They produce impediments to the more or less automatic flow of thought and lead on to exciting mind games and journeys. Brossardian words produce seisms in the apparently stable grounds of reality; they open spaces that readers quickly recognize as having to be opened, spaces that you probably hadn't previously known were available for imagination, fresh knowledge, emotion and experience. In these spaces words appear, like fragments of holograms, to be parts of wholes they already contain but will only reveal in certain lights:

> Ce sont des mots comme genou ou joue et encore d'autres à perte de vue qui nous obligent à nous pencher au-dessus du vide, à nous étirer comme des chats le matin ce sont des mots qui font veiller jusqu'à l'aube ou prendre un taxi les soirs de semaine quand la ville s'endort avant minuit et que la solitude reste coincée entre les mâchoires comme un abcès (CR 91).

> [It is words like knee or cheek and still others as far as the eye can see that oblige us to lean out over the void, to have a good stretch like cats in the morning it is words that make you stay awake until dawn or take a taxi on weeknights when the city falls asleep before midnight and solitude remains stuck between your jaws like an abscess.][2]

Brossard writes with urgency on the temporal and spatial margins of the modern city to resist dangerous abuses of power and to explore the limitless riches human imaginations can discover for themselves when words and bodies are free to circulate untram-

melled in as many dimensions as they wish, propelled
only by the energy of their own desire and sense of
wonder. This freedom of circulation that underlies her
modes of writing has often taken the *personae* and fictional characters who speak in her texts into realms
that shed new light onto all the vexing issues human
beings are prone to have to address in their lives and
that philosophers have debated for millennia, issues
that raise questions about the nature of love, beauty,
knowledge, truth, reality, time, space, memory, death,
dreams, fantasy, materiality, corporeality, solitude,
spirituality, cruelty and injustice. The uncharted and
unspoken spaces and dimensions where free human
bodies and spirits can roam at will are represented by
images of seas, deserts, aerial expanses, and the depths
of holograms that are in reality *surfaces of sense*. She
often situates her characters on edges where such
expanses meet civilization's realities.

The poet's voice reflected Brossard's identity as a
woman right from her earliest texts. This did not have
in the beginning, however, any particular social or
political significance in terms of the ways her texts produced meaning. She has said that in the 1960s and
early 1970s she believed that the poet's voice and message are neutral, unmodulated by the sex of the person
writing. She spoke of "le temps que je pensais comme
un homme" (*LA* 12) ["days when I thought like a
man" (*AL* 37)]. This view underwent a rapid change
around 1974, when feminist issues came to be central

in her writing. About the same time she fell in love with a woman and explicitly sited herself as a lesbian writer. For her, as for Daphne Marlatt, *to write in lesbian* does not mean making statements about lesbians in general. Rather, it involves putting words on pages that evoke the voice and corporeal presence of a woman in the world whose passions carry her toward another woman and other women. While the phenomenon is simple in itself, its impact on patriarchal cultural practice – when a woman represents both the range of her human relations and the source of meaning in her life as primarily focussed on and nurtured by women – is revolutionary. It is *heavy with consequences*.

Brossard's output since the 1970s as a lesbian writer exploring feminist concerns is incredibly rich and innovative. Her first explicitly feminist text was *Mécanique jongleuse*, suivi de *Masculin grammaticale*, in the title of which she made a deliberate grammatical error and so drew attention to the arbitrarily sexist rules of language norms. I have not encountered any previous examples of such transgressive play with the *mute e*, the signal of femininity by the conventions of French grammar. This approach of flaunting grammar rules in order to reveal the extent to which unacknowledged sexism is integral in the normal functioning of the words and syntax that form the basis of language usage was fully developed in 1975 in her explosive text "*E* muet mutant," ["Mute *E* Mutating"] where she rebelled against women's cultural invisibility as conse-

quential individuals and affirmed the power of writing
to produce cultural visibility, historical presence, and the
reality of women as subjects possessing agency: "Écrire
c'est se faire voir. [...] La femme qui écrit passe donc
enfin dans l'histoire [...] Elle devient sujet. Elle propose.
Impose son sujet – souvent celui de sa parole censurée"
(*DI* 55) ["Writing is making oneself visible. [...] The
woman who writes thus finally enters [...] She becomes
a subject. She proposes. *Imposes her subject* – often that
of her censored speech" [Ellipse 23/24 49, 51].

I don't know who first used the expression *l'écriture
au féminin [writing in the feminine]*, a term that is now
so widely used that its origin is no longer sought. I
believe, however, that this particular expression that
captures so well an exciting new approach to collective
feminist action emerged in the exchanges among the
group of Québec feminist writers with whom Brossard
was closely collaborating. Adoption of this expression
has been *heavy with consequences* for Brossard's creative
and reflective processes, for it is an approach to writing
whereby mind and body, fantasy and intellectual
rigour, fictional invention and theoretical analysis produce dazzling synergy. Alice Parker recently defined
writing in the feminine "as a textuality that emerges
from modernity, a woman's body and history combined with a feminist consciousness." Parker sees in
writing in the feminine the freedom "to explore the
junctures between gender, sexuality, subjectivity and
textuality" ("Surviving in Another Tongue" 50, 51).

Brossard was not using the expression *writing in the feminine* in 1975, despite the writing practice she was rapidly implementing and that we now recognise, without hesitation, as *écriture au féminin*. The expression which Brossard often used in "*E muet mutant*" to express the writing practice that she was inventing was *parler femme [speaking woman (DI 67)]*. In a text from the same year she writes, again evoking many of the aspects we associate with *writing in the feminine*: "Je parle par l'écrit à un autre sujet" (*AL* 23) ["I speak, by way of the written, to another subject" (*AL* 47)].

The first time that I encountered the expression *l'écriture au féminin* was when I heard Suzanne Lamy's conference paper "Voyage autour d'une écriture" ["Journey around a Writing"] at the Conference of Inter-American Women Writers in 1978, subsequently published in *d'elles* (53- 67). In this theoretical paper, she raised many questions and was clearly seeking theoretical expression for the sudden emergence of radical women's writing in France, Québec and elsewhere. She did not distinguish between *l'écriture au féminin* and the largely European phenomenon *l'écriture féminine*, from which it came to depart absolutely.

Nicole Brossard and others in Québec and France may well already have been using the expression *l'écriture au féminin*. In any case, as Brossard began to use it around 1978 to represent her own unique approach to writing, its semantic layers which made it possible to playfully superimpose multiple versions of reality were

immediately apparent. I suggest that its various mani-
festations in her writing show her to be, all at the same
time, a courageously militant public intellectual, an
original philosophical thinker, and a writer of some of
the most ecstatic and vertiginous love poetry – poetry
that celebrates and elicits women's unfettered *jouissance* – the world has ever known: "les écritures ont un
sens qui commencent par l'aveu d'amour" (*AM* 54)
["writings make sense that begin with the declaration
of love" (*L* 67)]. The words of her texts evoke in the
intensity of present moments the erotic and intellectual energy of women fully enjoying their own bodies,
their minds, their spirits and their place in the cities of
today, looking forward confidently toward tomorrow,
and claiming full ranges of memories for themselves:
"Tout corps porte en lui un projet de haute technologie
sensuelle; l'écriture en est son hologramme" (*LA* 45)
["All bodies carry within themselves a project of sensual high technology; writing is its hologram" (*AL* 68)].
Writing: I am a woman (and, simultaneously, *in the
feminine*) *is*, indeed, *heavy with consequences.*

Brossard's engagement with writing as a woman
has never been a solitary project. No …the heavy consequences which she foresaw at the time she wrote
These Our Mothers were consequences for all women
prepared to write and to read. At the same time that
Brossard has invoked rapid, multi-directional travel in
the vast inner spaces of one's own silence, imagination
and consciousness, she has collaborated with other

writers, with translators, with readers, with those who share her horror at events and practices produced by the realities of patriarchy, and has worked tirelessly to nurture the complicity among lucid, ardent women that will bring change:

> Je parle dans la perspective d'un pacte politique avec d'autres femmes. Touchez-moi. La vie privée est politique [...] J'écris et je ne veux plus faire cela toute seule. Je nous veux. Faire craquer, grincer, grincher l'histoire (*E* 74, 75).

> [As I speak, I have a political pact among women in mind. Touch me. Private life is political [...] I write and I don't want to do it alone any more. I want us. I want to make history shake and shudder and growl (*W* 34, 35).]

The erotic current of her words is a primal source of the energy that courses through her writing and that opens inner and outer spaces where imagination allows mind, body, and spirit to roam freely:

> Peut-être s'agit-il surtout de prendre un espace et de l'occuper. D'avoir l'oeil ouvert sur ce qui se passe et qui souvent nous dépasse faute d'interrogations, faute d'informations. Intervenir dans les rouages phallocratiques, ceux du pouvoir à côté d'elles et qui les concerne. [...] Intervenir donc dans cet ordre réducteur et avancer dans l'espace fictionnel, le terrain sans frontière prévisible de l'imaginaire, de la dérive en somme d'une énergie qui se dissémine (*La Barre du Jour*. 50: 23).

> Perhaps what matters most is to take a space and occupy it. To have our eyes open on what is going on and what often

goes right by us for lack of questioning, for lack of information. Intervening in the phallocratic gears, the powerful
ones that are right beside women and that concern them
[...] Intervening therefore in that reductive order and
advancing into fictional space, the terrain without foresee-
able borders of the imaginary, of moorings cast off in the
final analysis of an expanding energy.

Notes

1. This title is, of course, a borrowing with a difference from Nicole Brossard's won-
   derfully disruptive statement in *L'amèr/ These Our Mothers:* "Écrire: je suis une
   femme est plein de conséquences" (43) ["To write: I am a woman is heavy with
   consequences" (45)].
2. Here and elsewhere in "To Write," translations of works that have not previously
   been published in English are mine.

Works Cited

Bekenstein, Jacob D. "Are You a Hologram? Quantum Physics Says the Entire
    Universe Might Be." *Scientific American*. 289.2 (August 2003): 58-65.

Brand, Dionne. *Bread Out of Stone*. Toronto: Vintage Canada, 1998.

Lamy, Suzanne. "Voyage autour d'une écriture." *d'elles*. Montréal: Éditions de
    l'Hexagone, 1979. 53-60.

Marlatt, Daphne. "Booking Passage." *Salvage*. Red Deer: Red Deer College Press,
    1991. 111- 119.

Parker, Alice. "Surviving in Another Tongue: Nicole Brossard's *Installations*." *Verdure*
    5-6 (2002): 44-53.

Pizarnik, Alejandra. "In This Night, in This World." *Texts of Shadow and Last Poems*.
    Alejandra Pizarnik. A Profile. Ed. and Trans. Frank Graziano. Durango CO:
    Logbridge-Rhodes, 1987. 91- 2.

Since Yesterday
Nicole Brossard's Writing after Loss

Karen S. McPherson

Nicole Brossard's prose writings have always been marked by her resistance to narrative, her refusal of a transparent authorial *I*, and her lack of interest in indulging in "'the illusion of reality' that as readers we look for and inevitably find in novels" (Russo 125). Both her fictions and her more "autobiographical" writings have systematically challenged narrative conventions of referentiality and troubled the boundaries between fiction and nonfiction, character and author, poetry and prose, language and silence. Though she has acknowledged that women need prose "because they have so much to remember" (Russo 129) and prose offers "une façon de négocier avec la réalité" ["a way of negotiating with reality"], Brossard has nevertheless remained personally uneasy with "toute forme de témoignage, autobiographie, mémoire, journal intime, roman" ["any form of testimony, autobiography, memoir, diary, novel" (*ES* 18, 19)]. Over the years, however, Brossard's novels have become increasingly novelistic, and she has also produced several texts – notably *Journal intime*, *Oeuvre de chair et de métonymies*, and *Elle serait la première phrase de mon prochain roman* – that flirt rather shamelessly with the autobiographical mode. In addition, these more "personal" writings reflect and resonate with her fictional texts in revealing ways. Thus we find a passage in *Elle serait* self-consciously describing the author of *Mauve Desert* as seemingly "réconciliée avec la prose, à tout le moins, lui accorda[n]t plus de respect" (*DM* 10) ["reconciled with prose, or at the very least [...], showing it greater respect" (*MD* 11)]. Yet the authority of this potentially revealing statement is neatly undercut by the mode of its narration in the third person. Brossard's apparent "reconciliation" with prose is clearly an ongoing negotiation, as is her relationship with any autobiographical *I*.

Brossard has persisted in making prose out of her resistance to prose, opening up new possibilities for what prose is and what it can do. In *Mauve Desert,* the writing, reading and translating of the protagonist Melanie's story suggested the transformative potential of narrative. Telling and retelling, grounded in both imagination and desire, might offer a way of countering the violent ending. In *Baroque at Dawn*, Brossard again privileged what Alice Parker has so aptly described as "the corpo*reality* of her textual practice" (202). In that novel, the writing of the present and of presence in the context of a voyage through "virtual reality" inscribed the possibility, suggested in Brossard's own imbedded epigraph, that "[p]rose is a dream falling back into reality" (89, in English in the French text). The narrative projects of both *Mauve*

Desert and *Baroque at Dawn* furthermore resonate with Brossard's assertion in "Memory: Hologram of Desire" that women's future depends on the narration of memory: "Without an internal account, without narrative illumination, without its text, memory is an eater of destiny" (43). Finally, the ludic inscription of Brossard herself as a character in both *Baroque at Dawn* and *Elle serait* illustrates her idea that women may in fact need to "sort[ir] de la fiction par la fiction" ["exit fiction via fiction" (*ES* 98, 99)].

Brossard's most recent novel *Hier*, like *Mauve Desert* and *Baroque at Dawn*, consciously explores the transformative possibilities of women's engagement with history and story, as well as the vital role of both memory and narrative in opening up the possibility of survival and healing. But in *Hier*, the return to the personal voice of a *journal intime* – marked by the repetition of the word *"hier"* ("yesterday") – and that voice's significant claim on much of the narrative space in the novel are striking. Within *Hier*'s elaborate and shifting narrative construction, the reader is particularly moved by the urgency of a first-person narrator who is writing *since* (her narration punctuated by the refrain "depuis la mort de maman" ["since Mama's death"]). This narrator believes that "pour écrire, il faut au moins une fois dans sa vie avoir été traversé par une énergie dévastatrice, presque agonique" (13) ["in order to write, one must at least once in one's life have been pierced by a devastating, a nearly agonizing energy"].[1] If the earlier novels envisioned women's capacity – through writing – to "changer le cours de l'histoire" (*DM* 187, see also *BA* 123) ["change the course of history/the story" (My translation)] and even thereby perhaps "changer le cours de la mort" (220) ["change the course of death" (201)],[2] *Hier* reformulates this vision in more intimate terms, working its way towards a concluding sentence that makes a perhaps less ambitious but equally powerful claim:

> Tant mieux si l'écriture permet de détourner le cours des choses et d'irriguer là où le coeur est sec et demandant. C'est juste une petite phrase pour guérir (346).

> [So much the better if writing allows for *a shift in the course of things*, a watering there where the heart is parched and demanding. It is *just one small sentence for healing*" (emphasis mine).]

In its insistence on the persistence of loss and its acknowledgement of how loss touches and marks each individual, Brossard's latest novel defines the very personal stakes of both mourning and writing. And it is precisely in its modest suggestion that loss and healing may (need to) coexist that it is able to imagine a future.

Although the future symbolized by the horizon in *Mauve Desert* and the dawn in *Baroque at Dawn* is also evident in *Hier*, the emphasis seems to have shifted significantly towards connections to the past – an emphasis thematically evident in abundant references to museums, journals, ruins, relics, grandmothers, uncovered texts. The future is, nevertheless, contained within this perspective, for the focus is on the transformation of one's connections to the past into possibilities for survival. The "hier" of the text clearly signals this retrospective gesture, one that is both conservative (the *now* of telling trying to hang on to the *then* of experience) and visionary (for the narrative moves easily from "yesterday" to "since yesterday," and the sense of the present as still and always unfolding unquestionably brings the future into play).

Hier presents four women each with her own history and her own unfolding story and all struggling to situate themselves in relation to past losses. Simone Lambert, curator of the Musée de la Civilisation du Québec, is haunted by the death of her lover Alice and by the departure and loss of her daughter Lorraine; Saskatchewan novelist Carla Carlson comes to Quebec to write the stories of loss she has inherited from each of her parents; Simone's granddaughter Axelle Carnaval – through her scientific work in gene manipulation – seeks a way to deal with the loss of her parents; and the narrator *Je*, who works for Simone and whose job is to write the explanatory texts that accompany the museum exhibits, has been a compulsive note-taker and journal-writer since the recent death of her mother. The narrator makes explicit not only the fact that this kind of writing offers her a way not to be utterly subsumed by loss:

> Comme d'autres marchent allègrement vers la folie afin de rester vivants dans un monde stérile, je m'applique à vouloir conserver" (11).

> [While others are walking cheerfully towards madness in order to stay alive in a sterile world, I devote myself to trying to preserve.]

but also that such narrative *is* the writing of loss – haunting, painful, incomplete, inadequate:

> Il pleut depuis deux jours. *Hier* est un mot dont je fais mauvais usage. Depuis la mort de maman, je m'en sers contre le présent (27).

> [It's been raining for two days. *Yesterday* is a word I put to bad use. Since Mama's death, I use it against the present.]

In its weaving together of first-person narration with so many other kinds of "narrative" – third-person accounts, play scenarios, film scripts, taped conversations and their subsequent transcriptions, museum displays, translations, notebook jottings, authors' notes, stage directions – the novel both reveals its constructedness and confounds any simple attempt to locate and identify the source of that construction. The plotting and scripting of the contingent and yet incidental relationships among the four women is both that of the author Brossard and of her first-person narrator. Furthermore, the narrative performances in the novel are staged, not directed. Just as Brossard's narrator enjoys a large measure of autonomy, she in turn seems to give extensive creative agency to the other characters (so much so that her narrative presence is all but invisible in *their* sections of the novel). And the hybrid spaces of this novel set up the staging of identity as both narrative and performative – occurring both in the play of the text and in the text of the play (by which I mean, of course, the play, the film, the play within the film, and even the visit to the museum). But three key elements, familiar to any reader of Brossard's fiction, provide both thematic and textual continuity within these multiple and variable stagings: the scene of death, the scene of writing, and the gathering together of women. The scenes of death and of writing, by setting the stage for a consideration of the contours of identity, bring into focus the possibility of survival, healing, and the imagination of a future. Threaded through these scenes – and inseparable from them – are the encounters among women that seem always to be at the emotional centre of Brossard's writings.[3] Indeed, the need for such connection in response to the pervasiveness of loss seems particularly acute in Brossard's most recent writings.

Death intrudes frequently in *Hier*. The most striking instances may be the narrator's repeated references to her mother's dying: "Je ne pense jamais à ma mère de son vivant. Je ne la revois qu'à l'agonie ou morte mais encore chaude" ["I never think about my mother alive. I only see her in the throes of death or already dead but still warm" (27)]; the narrator's witnessing of the death of a dog: "Hier, en marchant sur les plaines d'Abraham, j'ai pris des notes pendant qu'un grand chien noir agonisait devant moi" ["Yesterday, walking on the Plains of Abraham I took notes while a large black dog was dying in front of me" (342)]; the news of Fabrice's murder that reaches Simone while she is visiting the museum: "Vingt-heure quatre minutes et dix secondes. La nouvelle est tombée dans le cellulaire de Simone Lambert comme un coup de hache sur l'oreille" ["Four minutes, ten seconds past eight o'clock. The breaking news on Simone Lambert's cell phone struck her ear like the blow of an ax" (212-13)]; or the subsequent inscription of Fabrice's death in the middle of one of the dramatic scenes as a black and inassimilable passage beginning with the words "trou noir" and closing with the words "trou noir impossible à enjamber" ["black hole impossible to step across" (228)]; and then, of course, there is the death of Descartes. Based on vivid memories of her childhood and "l'histoire inventée de la mort de Descartes" ["the invented story of Descartes' death" (93)] that was first her mother's obsessive fantasy and then her own, Carla has made this death scene the subject and substance of a crucial piece of her novel as well as of many of the conversations between her and the narrator. The story that is, for Carla, both inherited and adapted, both remembered and invented, becomes, in *Hier*, a central dramatic event, repeatedly narrated and then scripted and finally – when the four women come together in Carla's hotel room – acted out. Indeed, the staging of Descartes's death in the novel seems to function as a substitute and a screen for all the other deaths and losses that to some degree resist representation.

In the section called "La Chambre de Carla Carlson" ["Carla Carlson's Room" (269)], Carla the novelist becomes, within the cinematic space of the room, a dramatic narrator, first describing how she writes and rewrites her scenes, and then describing how they materialize around her until finally she is no longer narrating but acting. It is at this point that the text shifts (through an interpolated passage in italics that describes the scene about to be played) and offers us the staged scene of Descartes' dying – with Simone and the narrator in the roles of the Cardinal and Hélène and with Carla, tucked into the bed as Descartes, actually reciting all of the lines herself while the others mouth the words. In its placement and presentation within the text and above all in the fact of its being played in Latin, this staged scene seems to be first and foremost about its own staging. Is this what death is? A play in a foreign language? An intrusion on an ongoing conversation? An interruption of narrative? The scene is so strange and so compelling that one is forced to ask what it means and what it is doing. Why is Descartes of all people haunting not only Carla's text and consciousness but the text and consciousness of *Hier* as well? How does the imbedded and stylized death scene relate to or respond to the experiences of loss of the four women?

Carla's words give us some insight into her particular preoccupation with this scene. She writes of the dying Descartes:

> À lui seul, il représente toute une généalogie de penseurs, nouveaux et anciens, qui comme lui sont sur le point de souffler sur la chandelle brûlée à tout jamais par les deux bouts de la vie et de la mort" (316).

> [All on his own, he represents an entire genealogy of thinkers, modern and ancient, who like him are about to blow out the candle that has forever burned at both ends of life and of death.]

It is not Descartes dead, but Descartes *dying* that compels her – the fact of being, lucidly, on the point of blowing out the candle of one's own being. How better to interrogate being than to stage the encounter of being and nothingness? How could one resist wanting to see what happens when the man of *cogito ergo sum*, classic formula for defining identity, is going through that most exquisitely corporeal of experiences – dying? For the emphasis in this scene is on the philosopher's physicality and his human vulnerability: his desire to be touched and to see Hélène naked, his desire to write, to see his daughter (whose death he continues to deny), his cold, his thirst. The scene of Descartes's dying provides a certain theoretical catharsis within the novel's

economies of loss. At one point, Carla even momentarily confuses Descartes with her father, speaking about
"la bouche de papa, pardon de Descartes" ["Papa's
mouth, I mean, Descartes's" 94]. And the way in which
the deaths coincide and overlap is further suggested in
the narrator's remark that:

> Longtemps après la mort de maman et celle de Descartes,
> j'ai continué de noter comme si avec chaque mot je creu-
> sais un petit tunnel débouchant sur le mot univers .

> [Long after Mama's death and that of Descartes, I contin-
> ued to take notes as if with each word I was digging a little
> tunnel that opened onto the word universe (335).]

This key utterance which articulates an essential relationship between loss and writing occurs in *Chapter
Five* (327), the final section of the novel and the one
that most explicitly stages the scene of writing.
Interestingly, *Chapter Five* consists of two distinct parts.
The first eight-page section seems to continue the first-
person narrator's ongoing narration. But now, rather
than presenting itself under the sign of "yesterday"
with the immediate and unfolding quality of the *journal intime*, it offers – under its chapter heading – a
more considered, retrospective, summary narrative.
The voice, though still personal, is now that of a narrator who, in the last chapter, tells and reflects upon the
end of her story.

The other part of *Chapter Five*, however, reveals the

narrative scaffolding. This nine-page section, bearing the title "Quelques notes trouvées dans la chambre de l'Hôtel Clarendon" ["A Few Notes Found in the Hotel Room at the Clarendon" (337)], contains author's notes ostensibly written and left behind by the narrator (although, as is true of the entire chapter, this section is also problematic in its attribution – the content of the notes bears the mark of the narrator but the title points us to the hotel room that was in the previous section associated with Carla Carlson). *Chapter Five* (thus doubly organized around the scene of writing) inscribes the encounter between writing and death both in the way it structurally interrogates narrative endings and in the narrator's own imbedded conclusions – and inconclusions. The interrogation of narrative endings is initially suggested by the *open* ending of the previous chapter – its abrupt leap into empty narrative space that encouraged us to read *Chapter Five* as a possible alternative to the various cinematic and theatrical versions that went before. "Carla Carlson's Room" ended with the words:

> La narratrice vient se placer devant Carla qui disparaît ainsi que toute la scène dans le noir. Rideau. Ou (326).

> [The narrator comes to stand in front of Carla who disappears into darkness along with the entire scene. Curtain. Or]

What follows is then no longer performance but writing (and it is perhaps not surprising to find Brossard giving writing the last word). And yet the juxtaposition of constructed narrative and found notes in the final section also suggests a dynamic telling that is trying to survive its own disappearance.

Furthermore, *within* the narrative pages of this final chapter a powerful encounter between death and writing is played out as the narrator comes face to face with the fact that in responding to her loss through constant notation she has in fact been attempting to skirt or keep at bay the enormity and unskirtability of that loss. It is in the narrator's final self-accounting that the discontinuities and tensions between writing and living or dying are both revealed and enacted:

> J'ai pris des notes jusqu'à la fin sans m'apercevoir que la fin était arrivée. [...] Je prenais des notes et quelqu'un mourait au milieu des notes que je prenais (329).

> [I took notes until the end without noticing that the end had come. [...] I took notes and someone was dying in the middle of the notes that I was taking.]

It is not the staged death scene that intrudes here but rather that most personal loss that has haunted the narrator and the text from the start. Throughout the novel, the narrator's refrain of "since Mama's death" – with the unmistakable echo of Camus's *L'étranger* "Aujourd'hui, maman est morte. Ou peut-être hier" ["Today Mama died. Or perhaps yesterday"][4] – had both provided a certain narrative thrust and at the same time allowed the narrator to remain suspended somewhere between the past and the present. Now, in this final section, that refrain is suddenly inscribed as event: "the end had come," and the narrator realizes "Tout ce temps, quelqu'un mourait devant moi" ["All this time someone was dying in front of me" (333)]. This realization and this utterance break through the constructedness and narrative play of the novel. Here is that "black hole impossible to step across." But the narrator explains that she kept writing until the end because

> [...] je croyais pouvoir avancer dans l'indicible [... j] usqu'à la fin [...] de manière à pouvoir m'immobiliser dans le temps pour que vie résulte de vie (334).

> [I believed I could move forward in the unsayable [...] right up to the end [...] in such a way as to immobilize myself in time *so life might result from life.*]

Writing (after) loss is a paradoxical acceptance and refusal of its own impossibility. It is desire for, belief in, imagination of *after*.

In the closing paragraph of the narrative section of *Chapter Five*, even as she once again names the ending, the narrator resists concluding:

> Jusqu'à la fin, malgré la fatigue et le sommeil, j'ai cherché à comprendre ce qui était arrivé mais sans chercher à tirer une conclusion (336).

[Right up to the end, in spite of exhaustion and sleepiness, I sought to understand what had happened but without seeking to draw any conclusion.]

Thus she moves forward to occupy fully the *present* of her writing – "Aujourd'hui, je me tiens immobile devant le fleuve" ["Today I stand motionless before the river" (336)] – with her final sentence suggesting her continuing narration as she moves into the future: "je note tout ce qui pourrait passer pour une histoire" ["I take note of everything that might pass for a story" (336)]. The permeable boundaries between Brossard and her narrator allow them to share this final scene of writing. The notes – both found and left – fold back into the chapter which in turn folds back into the novel itself. The fact of this moving and shared narrative space brings back into dazzling focus the third central and unifying aspect of Brossard's vision in this novel, to which I earlier alluded: the gathering together of women, and the strong bonds of affection, identification and desire between and among them. The four women in *Hier* open up and inhabit this space – in their relationships with one another, with those others whom they are missing, *and* with their author. The narrator earlier insisted that she kept taking notes "pour revenir à l'idée d'un nous, d'une continuité au soleil" ["*in order to return to the idea of an us*, of a continuity in the sun" (my emphasis, 334)]. In the end, Brossard suggests, it is this vision of a connection between you and me and of a continuity between yesterday and tomorrow that may water the parched and demanding heart so that we may begin to survive our losses.

Notes

1. All translations of *Hier* are my own – KSM.

2. For further discussion of Brossard's treatment of this idea, see McPherson, Incriminations 176 and "Memory" 92, 100.

3. In *Elle serait,* Brossard describes how "l'écriture au féminin" ["writing in the feminine"] inscribes women's relation to one another: "C'est un concept dans lequel, le «je» intime et le «nous» de l'appartenance s'interpellent, cherchent à cohabiter malgré le sens patriarcal qui les isole pour mieux les invalider l'un et l'autre" (84) ["It is a concept in which the intimate "I" and the "we" of belonging gesture to each other and seek to cohabit despite patriarchal meaning that isolates them, the better to invalidate them both" (85).]

4. The opening lines ("Aujourd'hui maman est morte. Ou peut-être hier, je ne sais pas") of Camus's *L'étranger* are an important intertext for Brossard. In a passage in her *Journal intime,* she transformed them to read "Hier maman est morte" ["Yesterday Mama died"] and included this line as part of a litany of originary literary moments inscribing both loss and memory as signs of impending narrativity. The final line in that litany in Journal intime, "hier un texte qui commence ainsi" (54) ["yesterday, a text that begins that way" – my translation], anticipated and prefigured Brossard's project in *Hier* in provocative ways.

Works Cited

McPherson, Karen S. *Incriminations: Guilty Women/Telling Stories.* Princeton: Princeton UP, 1994.

———. "Memory and Imagination in the Writings of Nicole Brossard." *International Journal of Canadian Studies.* 22 (Fall 2000): 87-102.

Parker, Alice. *Liminal Visions of Nicole Brossard.* New York: Peter Lang, 1998.

Russo, Linda. "Sensational Intensities: Poetry and Prose: an Interview with Nicole Brossard." *Verdure.* 5-6 (February 2002):123-37.

Performativity in *Hier*

Alice A. Parker

Every language has its own dream language.

Ferenczi

Judith Butler locates the term *performativity* between linguistic determinants and dramatic performance (see Butler 1990, 1993, 1995, 1997). The concept relates back to speech act theory, to Austin's notion that words *do* things. Likewise, *performativity* draws upon psychoanalytic theory, which explains how early messages, experiences and phantasms govern behaviour (see Wright 1992). As well, one must factor in the poststructuralist critique of the voluntarist or epistemological subject, the pretensions of the subject that is self-governing and "presumed to know." Recent theory reconceives subjectivity as always/already subjected. Accordingly, intentionality (and political action) will consist in using the law against itself, in the resignification and redeployment of conventional discourses, which Nicole Brossard calls "ordinary," everyday wisdom.

Performativity is a sort of repetition compulsion that summons us to *do* things with the prescribed cultural messages, the roles (notably gender) and the language we have inherited. In response, Brossard's texts subvert conventional wisdom and practices, including the practice of writing. She uses repetition, reversal, silence and other narrative strategies to open space for the illegible, including lesbian desire. Faithful to her concept of the "cortex" (*corps/texte*), a corporeal writing, she blurs the boundaries between the body and the text, by giving voice to the unspeakable, for example, in *Hier*, the self-pleasure of masturbation and the agony of death. Thus she redraws the lines, not only of a normative subjectivity, who/what can count as a subject, but likewise of speech acts (see Butler 1997).

Hier, Brossard's tenth novel, presents a complex tale for four voices that blurs the boundaries between prose and poetry, narrative and drama, fiction and philosophy. Although there is only one narrator, omniscience is undermined by metatextual interventions and the juxtaposition of ontological locations. Brossard stages the experiences and virtual interactions of four women: Simone, a museum director who is an anthropologist/archaeologist; the narrator, her assistant; Carla, an anglophone writer who is the narrator's friend/lover; and Simone's granddaughter, Axelle. Three generations move us backward and forward in time, with (archaeological, historical and personal) memory adding even more depth. The scene is pointedly set in Québec City, pursuant to the writer's project to give cultural credence to her native land, although other geo-cultural locations come into play.

Brossard's double epigraph, the first from Gaston Miron, sets the tone: "Personne n'y peut rien/ mais les

objets mais les choses / personne personne / mais il
était une fois toutes les fois / jamais toujours et pour-
tant" ["There is nothing anyone can do/ but objects but
things / no one no one/ but once upon a time every
time / never always and however"].[1]

Subjectivity is difficult to seize, caught as it is
between perception, materiality and the fluidity of
time.

The second epigraph is a brief quote in French
from Alejandra Pizarnik: "Il faut sauver le vent" ["We
must save the wind"]. If the wind represents the breath
of the earth and by extension human breath that
anchors life itself and poetry, the project to "save" it is
urgent. *Hier* will thematize time, culture and preservation. Like all poets, Brossard is enchanted by paradox;
she delights in unlikely juxtapositions that force the
reader to reimagine figures of speech and semiosis.

The five-part text of her new fiction explores temporality as it affects concepts of mortality and family
relations, of continuity and change, finally the meanings of civilization itself. The most obvious modality of
prose fiction is how it deals with time. As Carla
observes, "Il faut laisser le temps circuler entre les personnages" ["you have to let time circulate among the
characters"]. The novel, she says, "n'est rien d'autre
que du temps décomposé qui retombe sur nos épaules
avec des allures de première neige et de poussières
douces" ["is nothing other than time decomposed
which falls back on our shoulders with the lure of the

first snow and gentle particles of dust" (149)]. Time, we have learned, is not linear but inseparable from the dimension of space, following principles of relativity. As always, Brossard is interested in process, in the shifting contours of time, space and e-motion. On his return from Venice, recounting his adventures, Fabrice notes the importance of transformativity: "'Changer de siècle, changer de sexe, changer de nom, tout changer dans une vie sans changer le verbe'" ["'Changing centuries, changing sex, changing your name, changing everything in your life without changing the verb'" (148). The verb is the pivot upon which everything turns.

According to performativity theory, each time a word, a phrase, a gesture is redeployed, normative values and practices can be transmuted and resignification can occur. *Hier* is perhaps the most millennial of Brossard's texts, even more pointedly so than *Baroque at Dawn*. At the edge of a new millennium and century, it is time to interrogate where we have been, where we are going, what the present holds for us, to inquire into the lasting lessons of modernity. Performativity is secured in the fiction through various representational devices, structural divisions incorporating the ever-important element of silence, thematic repetition of scenarios of death and desire, (re)enactments of poignant moments from the characters' past that erase the boundaries between past and present, memory and culture. With Swedish, Italian, English and especially

Latin phrases in the text, Brossard continues to explore translation theory and code- switching. Often overcharged with meaning, words and gestures overflow their performative limitations as (re)citations, discharging unexpected energy into the text. As Derrida suggests, the *force* of the utterance is secured when it is severed from established contexts (Butler 1997:141). "[…U]nmoored from prior context," the name may become "an instrument of resistance in the redeployment that destroys the prior territory of its operation" (Butler 1997:163). The writer can create a "future of language" (and of subjects) by exploiting "the presuppositions of speech," which constitute the normativity that produces us as (legitimate) subjects (Butler 1997:140, 135).

Readers of *Hier* will recognize familiar Brossardian themes and figures: writers and writing, desire, art and beauty (in the feminine), vertigo and the horizon, hyperspace and scientific visions that leave an open field for invention and discovery. The narrator wonders if archaeological metaphors can help elucidate personal history and the history of ideas:

> Peut-on parler de ruines intérieures […] de ruines philosophiques? Il m'arrive parfois d'imaginer mes contemporains circulant, bras ballants, entre des idéologies tombées en ruines, capables enfin de les observer sous leurs angles les plus remarquables et les plus sombres (77).

> Can we speak of interior ruins […] of philosophical ruins?

> I sometimes imagine my contemporaries circulating, with dangling arms, between ideologies fallen into ruin, capable, finally, of observing them closely from their most remarkable and sombre angles.

Memory, Brossard wrote in *The Aerial Letter*, is a *hologram* of desire. Such a figure would suggest that desire, generated by voluntary and involuntary exercises of memory, invests memory with a polysemic emotional tonality, as well as a potential for imaginative, creative (re)combinations. Given the quantity and complexity of the perceptual data we store away in a lifetime, not to mention the lifetime of a culture, the possibilities are endless. What about memories that literally stop us dead, Axelle wonders: "Qu'est-ce qu'une image du passé quand elle vous arrête, lève la main et dit avec autorité: on ne passe pas? Faut-il la contourner en douceur, rebrousser chemin ou foncer vers elle à toute vitesse?" ["What about an image of the past that makes you stop, raises its hand and states with authority: you cannot pass? Should you quietly go around it, go back, or drive on at top speed?"(144)]. Brossard's recent work charts the performative dynamics of such memory work, deploying the resources of her cultural and literary heritage, the discursive, rhetorical and semiotic riches of the language. To use another of her figures, she invests in a *differential equation* of memory and desire, including those elements that have been consciously or unconsciously repressed but which continue to haunt the borders of our imaginary. These liminal materials, which she calls the *inédit* (the illegible/unspeakable), must be translated into known codes by words and by silences, by various representational practices.

As always, the writer provides a self-reflective/reflexive exercise in writing, in language and the sensual attraction of words and thought. *Hier* sets in motion the performative potential of linguistic/semiotic constructions, while deconstructing the cultural myths that hamper experimentation, the phantasms that hold us captive. As the writer jumps ontological levels from author to writer to narrator to characters, both onstage and offstage, the reader is immersed in the writing process, the play within the play, navigating the often obsessive interaction of memory and desire. The narrator is haunted by her mother's last moments, Carla by the drama of Descartes's agony and death, a "story" her mother imprinted on her psyche when she was just a child, which she has been reenacting since then. This drama permits her to reconnect with her forebears, her father's Sweden and the great plains of her childhood, scenarios she will rewrite for her novel. This (personal/cultural) memory work will likewise colour her interaction with the city of Québec and with her lover. Why, one wonders, *Descartes*? What possible meaning(s) does such a tale (such an icon?) hold for the Québec of the new millennium?

Cartesian thought continued to influence western metaphysics and francophone culture well into the

twentieth century. His struggle against the orthodoxy
of his time is likewise symbolic. This is old stuff
indeed, but recontextualized here like the artifacts
Simone used to unearth and which now she displays in
her latest exhibit. Such archaeological and genealogical
study not only has the potential to tease out new meanings, but also offers a technology of memory/desire;
each alternative scenario incorporates new details of
time past, highlights particular moments, inflected
with various permutations of desire. Brossard chooses
to restage the final moments of the philosopher's life,
his passage from the material realm and those who
might have been attendant upon this primal mystery, a
woman who might have been his wife or his daughter
and a cardinal modelled on a painting of Francis
Bacon. Significantly, the drama is filtered through the
consciousness and sensibility of Carla and her mother,
recounted, re-cited, re-enacted, refracted through the
lens of gender as one scenario follows another.

The text is divided into sections of varying lengths,
separated by ample white space. Here the reader can
mull over what has preceded and imagine what will
follow. As on a canvas, a good deal may be happening
in the blank spaces that the eye cannot yet register,
encoding unspoken or unwritten messages. Brossard
takes great care with the physical design of her texts.
There are four named portions, the first and longest
called "Yesterday," the brief "Urns," "The Clarendon
Hotel," and "Clara's Room," with a brief conclusion

called "Chapter 5." First-person narration alternates with third-person, exposition with dramatic interludes. Interspersed is a recurring message to an unknown lover, discovered by accident in the museum library. Brossard gives us a complex tapestry of voices, subverting traditional techniques. The effect is of a series of hyperlinks, permitting the reader to move back and forth through the text and in time and space. The kaleidoscopic narrative bridges the distance between generations and characters, between literature and painting, creating a "béance érotico-sémantique" ["erotico-semantic gap" (113)]. Here the physical pleasure produced by writing becomes indistinguishable from erotic excitement, the *jouissance* of the *sexte*, the *stexe*.

Like Roland Barthes and the theorists who followed, Brossard has consistently linked the exhilaration of artistic creation to that of (especially lesbian) lovemaking. She is the poet of desire in all of its permutations, in its transmutability. Desire and its many histories drives her narratives, transforming even the death of Descartes into a passion play. Juxtaposed to accounts of the characters' personal lives and work experiences, purposefully intertwined, is the sheet of paper the narrator has found in a book on diamond cutting … a page from a personal journal or a work of fiction? Inserted five times into the narrative, the sensuous, evocative words echo like a refrain, which takes on new meanings with each verse.

In fact, multiple losses occupy the stage in *Hier* in addition to the two referred to above (the deaths of Descartes and of the narrator's mother): deaths of Simone's lover, Alice; of Fabrice, the museum curator, a gay man and friend of the narrator; the losses of Carla's father; the disappearance of Simone's daughter, Axelle's mother; the agony of an unidentified black dog. Each of the characters has experienced significant losses and will replay scenes that help them understand the sources of their grief. However, this is not a sad or (psychologically) troubling text. As in other works, Brossard distances herself from traditional narrative techniques, eschewing causality and linearity. Rather, we find ourselves in a mythic dimension, with characters who, like the gods, speak in riddles, prophetically, for our instruction, so we can learn to think better and not expect the truth to be simple or convenient. Thus the grief work links us to art, civilization, eternity. After the death of her mother, the narrator feels the need to recenter, to reaffirm the joyful grounding of her life in Québec and her work:

> J'imagine qu'il faut la joie à propos de tout pour s'engouffrer dans le temps et le laisser se refermer sur nous. Oui, il faut sans doute laisser avaler le silence et les récits multiformes qui nous entourent comme une haie de roses (140-41).

> I imagine that joy is necessary for everything, to be engulfed in time and let it close back over us. Yes, it is doubtless necessary to let time swallow silence and the multiform stories that surround us like a hedge of roses.

The stage expands as the scene shifts from Québec City
to Montréal to the plains of western Canada to Sweden
to Mexico, Venice, Delos/Greece, Istanbul and the
Bosphorus and back, to the banks of the mighty St.
Lawrence river at the edge of the continent where it
joins the ocean. The real drama is located between the
characters' thoughts and emotions and the search for
the most meaningful words to translate their personal/
cultural location in relation to events and each other.

How does one confront "a sterile world" (11) where
triviality prevails and even war news appears daily in
the mouths of television personalities as an ongoing
fiction? The narrator's response is to focus on objects,
on preservation, on reading, looking around, staying
present (11- 12). Some mornings her voice is lost in "le
plein plaisir de naviguer entre les secondes" ["the pure
pleasure of "navigating between seconds" (11)].
Simone, her assistant, and Carla are lovers of words
and books, of past lives as well as artifacts that bear witness to the survival of culture. Words "enflame" her,
the narrator declares, even the minimal descriptions
she invents for the objects in the exhibition. Simone
ponders the words of Marie Guyart, Marie de
l'Incarnation as she dreams of seventeenth-century
New France and of her lover with whom she shared so
many experiences at distant sites. Juxtaposed are "real"
and imagined memories, ritually (re)enacted.

Brossard's texts have consistently challenged literary conventions, in favour of a free textuality. The ongoing discussion of Carla's novel provides a sort of virtual fiction. Further, *Hier* brings the limits of prose narrative and meta-narrative to crisis: the last part of the text exceeds its constraints, transmuting into a theatrical dénouement. The shift in focus allows the writer to focus more sharply on the characters, their interactions and the textual problems she has confronted in the course of the fiction. Likewise, the drama of the final portion of the text alters the perspective and the tonality, creates more intensity. The work thus not only juxtaposes ontological and epistemological levels, problematizing who we can be and what can be known, but reads like a mixed-media production, with the spontaneity of a happening and the depth of a philosophical voyage.

How can we be, as Simone suggests, "responsable devant l'histoire, ne pas la laisser nous engloutir dans l'oubli" ["responsible to history, not let it lull us into forgetfulness" (16)]? Is civilization, then, the gleam of time from within time (15), or "ces éclats de deuil" ["those bursts of grief" (17)] that haunt us as Fabrice believes? How can we explain the sensual passion that any art lover feels at the sight of artifacts from another age (17)? The new exhibit, *Siècles lointains [Distant Centuries]*, elicits personal and collective memories, enough to dream upon for those whose difficult, painstaking work made it possible and for the public to whom the gift of civilization is offered. Museums grant us not only a space for wonder, a reprieve from the drudgery of "the quotidian," but a glimpse of eternity, time in another dimension that turns the repetitions of daily existence against themselves.

Time conjures up a variety of associations: vestiges and vertigo (240), ruins past and present, joy and mourning, hope and loss, anticipation and preservation, history and the arts, the reminders and the traces, the prospect of our own ruins that project us into a virtual future (160). New apprehensions affect our understanding of subjectivity. Axelle is certain that there is "un moi virtuel" ["a virtual self" (244)] that may permit us to escape ourself. The ludic effect of masks can also cancel the effects of time (244-45). Writing allows one to "cheat on reality," to change places, to recontextualize themes – like grief – and characters, to disarm suffering, to inhabit a painting of Francis Bacon (248-49), whose work, like the obsessive memories, haunts the text.

Brossard brings the four major characters together in the third and fourth parts, first in a hotel bar and finally in Carla's room, the scene of writing as well as of lesbian desire and comradery. As in *Baroque at Dawn*, the hotel room here has a privileged status as a space of work, of transition, of significant encounters. More concrete than cyberspace, what better topos than the hotel for such postmodern concepts as provisional identities, multiple, overlapping subjectivities, simulation, shifting boundaries et al.? It is the perfect refuge from the fiction of the "real world," from simple truths and prepackaged junk thought. In the hotel room "no one" can become *anyone*, just as in the refurbished museum art objects from the past can find new surroundings, acquire new readings. And Carla can finish her novel.

In the end, nothing is resolved, especially between Simone and Axelle, who must bridge the gap left by an absent daughter and mother; words spoken are cryptic, barely touching the surface of a possible understanding. This is not any more tragic than the losses each has suffered. Each of the speakers is discreet, careful not to breach the boundaries of the other, but the future of such strong women, whom Brossard referred to early as "urban Amazons," is not in doubt.[3] They are survivors who will continue to do their work, on the side of civilization and desire.

Like the hotel room, the museum is a space for transitory installations. It provides a venue for the recitation of history and art, for virtual links to the past, for moving exhibitions. There are many ways of resisting the laws of the fathers (of the Church, of philosophy, of the nation); Brossard's work reflects her passion for living, for writing, for beauty, for the present. But she never forgets the violence that is just around the corner, as we saw earlier in *Mauve Desert*, in texts on the massacre at Polytechnique, in *Baroque at Dawn*, in her theoretical writing and poetry. We have to stay present in spite of the lure of yesterday or tomorrow (95), in spite of the "fosses communes" ["common graves" (95)] of daily stupidity.

Discourses that maintain the status quo depend on iterability, the replication of cultural messages. Brossard is always working against this system in order to redefine language practice and meanings, gender and sexuality. Performativity theory and psychoanalysis teach us that speech acts always conjure up more than they say, especially in combination with body language. Thus conscious acts of re-signification have the potential to alter subjectivity, agency, power and politics. In Carla's novel and in the fiction we are reading, Descartes dies a new death each time; Queen Cristina plays new roles; Simone and her helpers reread/reinterpret history; the lesbian lovers and Fabrice trace new sexual/affective modalities; memory is recreated with an expanded understanding of generations and family; the language takes on new tonalities; the world assumes new colours and time itself morphs into uncanny virtualities.

Thus, like the writers she admires Nicole Brossard sets out to "save the wind," playing between the spaces of " ...once upon a time every time / never always and however." Through characters that seem to assume mythic proportions, we stage our own inquiries into where we have been, how/where we are going. Meanings in the brossardian oeuvre are layered, polysemic, multidimensional: *Hier* is both present and virtual, as are today and tomorrow.

Notes

1. All translations from Hier and other texts are my own – A.P.

2. *Sexte* is a term Hélène Cixous put into circulation in her landmark essay, "The Laugh of the Medusa," first published as "Le Rire de la Méduse" in *L'Arc* in 1975. Combining *sex* and *text,* it is analogous to Brossard's use of **cortex,** although the latter is more comprehensive, implying a body-writing. In *Hier* Brossard uses the term *stexe* (49 and passim).

3. Throughout her oeuvre, Brossard associates writing, indeed creative effort, at once with the city and with a *utopian, generic, aerial, radical* (lesbian) woman. (See especially *Picture Theory* and *The Aerial Letter.*) As she wrote in *These Our Mothers,* and has since often repeated: "Écrire: je suis une femme est plein de conséquences" (43) ["To write: I am a woman is heavy with consequences" (45)].

Works Cited

Austin, J.L. *How to Do Things with Words.* 2nd Ed. Cambridge, MA: Harvard UP, 1975.

Butler, Judith. *Bodies That Matter: On the Discursive Limitations of Sex.* New York: Routledge, 1993.

——. *Excitable Speech: A Politics of the Performative.* New York: Routledge, 1997.

——, with Seyla Benhabib, Drucilla Cornell and Nancy Fraser. *Feminist Contentions: A Philosophical Exchange.* New York: Routledge, 1995.

——. *Gender Trouble: Feminism and the Subversion of Identity.* New York: Routledge, 1990 & 1999.

Cixous, Hélène Cixous. "The Laugh of the Medusa." *New French Feminisms.* Eds. Elaine Marks and Isabelle de Courtivron. New York: Schocken Books, 1981. 245-64.

Wright, Elizabeth, Ed. *Feminism and Psychoanalysis: A Critical Dictionary.* Oxford: Basil Blackwell, 1992.

Novels on the Edge

Louise Dupré

The notion of *genre* in literature has been significantly shaken in recent decades, to the point that the novel's boundaries have become very porous today.[1] This challenge to tradition has often been thrown out by women. Scholars have not failed to draw attention to the link between literary genre and *gender*. Evidence in Québec for this phenomenon is provided by what I shall call the novel *au féminin*, that is, the novel developed by Québécoises who explored women's subjectivity while inscribing it in textuality. The modernist poets publishing during the 1970s in two important literary magazines in Québec, *La Barre du Jour* and *Les Herbes Rouges*, sought to abolish the boundaries between poetry and prose, narrative, the personal journal, the epistolary, theoretical reflection, and sometimes even dramatic writing. The women among them collaborated extensively in redefining the field of poetry by mainstreaming a sub-genre that had remained marginal until then in Québec: prose poetry.

In "La séduction du romanesque" ["The seduction of the novelistic"], an interesting special section in *Estuaire,* Gerald Gaudet noted a profound attraction toward the novelistic in the poetry of the 1980s. Yet, although it may have been less evident, this temptation was already being felt in the texts of the 1970s, more particularly in the works of women writers who were attracted by feminism and who felt the need to commit feminine history to writing, considered minor and passed over until then. It is not surprising that this prose poetry hybrid should have led them to a deliberately narrative prose. Nicole Brossard, Madeleine Gagnon, France Théoret, Carole Massé, Geneviève Amyot, and then later Louise Desjardins, Élise Turcotte, Christiane Frenette, Rachel Leclerc, among others, crossed the threshold that took them to the side of the novelistic, while in parallel they continued to publish collections of poetry.

But it was a revamped and revisioned novel form that these poets' novels present. They engage us in a reading that is different from that evoked by novelists' novels, to use a pleonasm. When we look at them carefully, we realize that even if these texts offer a plot, it is tenuous and remains secondary. These novels place a voice in the foreground, an intimate, inner voice that whispers, murmurs, chants, sings, or shouts, occasionally roars, but which always seeks to give witness to a vision of the subjective, personal world. Poets' novels are, in effect, novels of the voice.

Nicole Brossard's Novel Hier

This is what we encounter in *Hier*, Brossard's most recent novel. This complex novel, where four women meet, weaves theatrical scenes and notes into the narration. Narration in the third person alternates with narration in the first person. And then we discover that we are dealing with a novel within the novel, in any case a text for which responsibility is taken by a *je/I* who is called the narrator and who offers her thoughts on writing in the final notes. Between this narrator who claims the story and the *persona* of the author, we observe a subtle play of mirrors. This is a frequent technique in the postmodern novel. Even if *Hier* presents greater complexity than other poetic novels published today in Québec, it belongs to this sub-genre. Usually speaking in the first person, the narrator of these novels makes herself heard, less to tell a story leading to a dénouement than to give readers her point of view on the world. The opening lines of *Hier* are very revealing in this regard:

> Comme d'autres marchent allègrement vers la folie afin de rester vivants dans un monde stérile, je m'applique à vouloir conserver. Je m'accroche aux objets, à leur description, à la mémoire de paysages tout entier dessinés dans les plis des choses qui m'entourent. Chaque instant me requiert, regard ou sensation (11).

> As others are walking cheerfully toward madness in order to stay alive in a sterile world, I am trying to preserve. I latch on to objects, to the description of them, to the memory of landscapes totally outlined in the folds of the things that surround me. Every moment summons me, with a look or sensation.

This gives the tone straight off, an intimate tone of witnessing on the part of the *I*, who will reveal herself as feminine in the second paragraph when she says: "J'ai grandi entourée..." ["I grew up surrounded..." (11)]. Right from the start, the speaker isolates herself: there are those who "marchent allègrement vers la folie," the movers, and she who observes and describes. Thus appears a universe where two opposing series are in place: those who are agitated on one side and she, the contemplator, on the other; on the one side those who try to forget the sterility of the world by plunging into the madness of an empty temporality, and on the other, she, who is trying to remain sensible and who, to that end, is working on "la mémoire des paysages" by stopping time and by committing the slightest moment to writing. This can be seen in the statement: "Chaque instant me requiert."

Unlike novels which also *are walking* toward their end, poems display a temporality outside of any progression. They introduce a break in historical linearity. This suspended, "arrested" present can be associated with what Benjamin calls *Jetzzeit*, l'*à-présent*, the *a-present*, that "figure un temps intensif, qualitatif, celui [...] où la mémoire refoulée des 'sans-noms' (*Namenlosen*) se réapproprie enfin une histoire dominée par l'historicisme des puissants" (Buci- Glucksmann: 22), "represents a qualitative, intensive time, a time [...] in which the suppressed memory of the nameless

(*Namenlosen*) finally reappropriates for itself a history dominated by the historicism of the powerful." Benjamin's vision finds a direct echo in the enterprise of these women poets who, influenced by feminism, sought to break patriarchal hegemony in order to reinscribe a memory of the feminine. Writing this way becomes a deliberate political act, as is the case for Nicole Brossard. I am reminded of the statement in *These Our Mothers*, so often cited: "Écrire: je suis une femme est plein de conséquences" ["To write: I am a woman is heavy with consequences" (45)].

Even if the political vision is no longer as explicit in Nicole Brossard's recent books, it subtends all her work since 1975. The novel *Hier* is no exception to this, as is shown by the speaking protagonist who expresses her desire to prevent the repression of little facts of memory. As we have seen, attaching herself to the "folds of things," she admits: "Je ne me départis pas facilement des jours en les reléguant dans le livre des blancs de mémoire" ["It isn't easy for me to let go of days by relegating them to the book of memory losses" (11)]. That is her project: to act in such a way that the moment is not lost, is not swallowed by the horizontality of History. Instead, she introduces a verticality, a piling up of moments that creates for her, and for us as readers, a presence in the world.

This is not to say that there is no action in *Hier*. In fact, the second chapter begins with the sentence "Hier, j'ai marché longtemps" ["Yesterday I walked for a long time" (13)], as if to immediately contradict what was presented in the first chapter. But there is a lot of walking in Québec poetry: Saint-Denys Garneau, Gaston Miron and, closer to us, France Théoret, are great walkers.[2] The protagonist of Nicole Brossard's novel is referring to this type of poetic *flânerie*. It is a matter of slowly sauntering, meandering, or idling, thus provoking a revelation, rather than heading toward a precise point. Joining a group of women demonstrating on the first of May, the narrator of the novel *Hier* allows herself to drift in their flow and no longer know where she has come. This situation reminds her of lost children in films of war and leads, through an association of ideas, to a reflection on war: "Je pense souvent à la guerre, mais comme on pense à manger un biscuit soda. Je veux dire j'oublie vite que je viens de penser à la guerre" ["I often think about war, but it's like thinking about eating a soda biscuit. I mean I quickly forget that I have just thought about war" (13)].

Here the movement of walking has no narrative consequences; instead, it engenders a self- critical observation on the part of the narrator, who does not live war from the inside, being content to observe it from the outside. Besides, it is not a matter of one war in particular, but of all wars in the world which end up forming the general image of war, detached from any specific temporal and spatial context. And so temporality exceeds the borders of time. The narrator is conscious of this in her affirmation, once more through an association of ideas: "Le temps luit dans le temps" ["Time is glowing in time" (15)]. Nothing prepared the reader for this statement.

The Characters

This anchoring in a timeless present is based upon characters who also inscribe themselves in a present moment outside of time. It is not that they have no past: we know, for example, that the narrator has lost her mother. Simone Lambert has a daughter and a granddaughter, Axelle, who spent her childhood abroad and is returning to live in Montréal. Carla was raised in the Plains of the Canadian West. But the personal history of the characters does not give them the psychological density found in the traditional novel. They seem to be neither marked by their past nor marching toward the future. They are there, for a moment, the time of an encounter, and it is not by chance that the text finally develops into a long conversation taking the form of a theatrical dialogue among the characters, in a room of the Hotel Clarendon in Québec City, as if the temporal flow of the story had reached a point of fixing itself definitively, at the end of the novel, in the present – the *presence* – of the dramatic scene.

Characters in *Hier* are beings whose form is determined by their gaze on the world, by their own reflections; they are not subjects of a quest they are trying to undertake through actions, but of a thought, a questioning. They distinguish themselves clearly from the characters of the usual novel "who are walking cheerfully toward madness": in order to remain alive they seize the moment in a spiralling descent to the centre of themselves. This means that, like the protagonists of Nicole Brossard's earlier novels, characters in *Hier* do not try to become beings of flesh and blood but, to borrow a term from Jean-Yves Tadié, they are "créature[s] de langage, née[s] des mots et qui vi[ven]t par les mots" ["creatures of language, born from the words, and living through the words" (27)]. They are created in the present through the process of enunciation, a process also in the present.

But if the characters do not have psychological depth, in the sense this is normally understood in the novel, they still show a high degree of complexity in their questioning. In fact, they are like the enunciating voice in prose poetry. Brossardian characters achieve in effect the status of rhetorical figures, depersonalised figures who, whatever their social situation in the novel, achieve universality: they becomes archetypes of contemporary women, new symbols, modern myths. After the Mother in the home entirely devoted to her children who could be seen in traditional Québec literature, here we encounter an image of women who want to be lovers, mothers, intellectuals and creators all at the same time.

What is more, we have the impression that the three

women of mature age in the novel represent versants of the same woman, a contemporary woman who questions herself in order to rethink civilization's values. One woman and, at the same time, all women who pause a moment to reflect. This is a characteristic of the lyric subject. As Dominique Combe notes in "La référence dédoublée: Le sujet lyrique entre fiction et autobiographie," the lyric or poetic *I* is neither autobiographical nor fictional, but a subject who tends toward generalisation and universalisation, who "s'élargit jusqu'à signifier un 'Nous' inclusif large" ["expands to the point of signifying a broad, inclusive 'We'" (57)].

This fact becomes particularly obvious in the chapters for which the narrator takes responsibility, where the tonality of the voice comes close to the one heard in recent collections of prose poetry by Nicole Brossard:

> Je ne sais pas grand-chose de la douleur, mais j'ai la certitude que pour écrire, il faut au moins une fois dans sa vie avoir été traversé par une énergie dévastatrice, presque agonique. Je n'aime pas beaucoup employer le mot agonie. Depuis la mort de maman, je sais ce que cela signifie chercher son souffle, avoir le soi enfermé dans de petites veines bleues qui font penser à des papillons sur le point de partir au loin [...] Les mots m'enflamment (13-14).

> I don't know a great deal about suffering, but I'm certain that in order to write you must have been traversed at least once in your life by a devastating energy, almost death-like agony. I don't like to use the word agony very much. Since mother's death I know what it means to try to catch your breath, to have yourself enclosed in little blue veins that

suggest butterflies on the verge of going far away [...]
Words set me on fire.

In the novel *Hier*, an intimate voice can be felt, corre-
sponding to this *"Je* est un autre" ["*I* is another"] that
individuals inevitably encounter in themselves when
they plunge into their own identity.[3] Subjects create
themselves in language and so create through fiction
some possibilities for agency. Thus, the narrator allows
herself to be inflamed by words. They incite her to cast
herself adrift, to enter into a system where literal meaning is constantly deflected toward simile or metaphor.
A mythical figure, as I have already stated, the narrator
speaks figuratively, as is characteristic of poetic language, where the paradigmatic axis of language
expands beyond the horizontal, syntactic axis to construct layers of linguistic verticality.

Poetic Structure

Those who have even passing familiarity with Nicole
Brossard's poetic works will know that this search at
the heart of language is not surprising at all. Her
approaches to poetry and to the novel derive from a
common vision. In this, as Jean-Yves Tadié reminds us:

> [...] la déréalisation, le renoncement à l'illusion référen-
> tielle [chez le personnage] attirent encore davantage l'at-
> tention sur la structure poétique, proprement verbale, du
> message transmis. Les voix qui parlent, et surtout celle du
> protagoniste, les images humaines qui passent ne sont pas

très différentes de celles qu'on rencontre chez Éluard ou Saint-John Perse. [...] [l]e vide sémantique du personnage fait le plein du texte" (45).

[...] the de-realisation, the renunciation of the referential illusion [in the character] draw even more attention to the strictly verbal, poetic structure of the transmitted message. The voices that speak, and especially the protagonist's, the human images that pass are not very different from those found in Éluard or Saint-John Perse [...] the character's semantic void makes the fullness of the text.

This observation is fitting for the novel *Hier*, a language novel. Like a poem, its structure functions by displacement, condensation and overdetermination. The characters are caught in the movement of a reflection often miming the drifting of a thought which, in turn, finds its focus in poetic writing where it is the trope that dominates. This is not the verisimilitude of the traditional novel. Yet even if *Hier* does not try to create a referential illusion, this does not mean that the Brossardian character represents the semantic void toward which the usual poetic account tends. In fact, the enterprise of Québec women writers since the 1970s has consisted less in showing the semantic void than in working from a starting point of negativity so as to create in fiction some possibilities for agency. Recognizing that, even recently in literary tradition, female characters has been identified with a semantic void, which can be seen for example in André Breton's Nadja or often in Marguerite Duras's women, these writers take this void as a starting point and work their way into a mobile and supple subjectivity in action.

Nicole Brossard works to ensure that the female character becomes an agent, and that she finds within herself the thoughts she needs to nourish her. Brossard is aware of the fact that it is the "fullness of language" which creates the volume needed to bring the *I* into existence. If "le sujet lyrique se crée dans et par le poème, qui a une valeur performative" ["the lyric subject creates itself in and through the poem, which has a performative value"], as Combe states (63), it does the same thing in and through the novel. Thus characters undertake textual quests, not following Propp's actantial model, that is through the novel's action, but through the invention of figures of women who imbed themselves in textuality and so make modification of the symbolic order possible.

Thus, the narrator of *Hier* – like the other characters Carla, Simone or Axelle – seeks to give a centre to her life, and beyond that, to life generally in a contemporary world in complete disarray. She affirms:

> J'ai parfois l'impression de marcher sur un plancher de verre transparent où les grands principes humanistes forment une passerelle étroite sans garde-fou qu'il faut obligatoirement traverser en prétextant ne pas avoir peur ni vertige. Avancer dans la vie, les poings fermés, les yeux terriblement savants et vibrant d'identité (71).

> Sometimes I have the impression I'm walking on a transparent glass floor where the great principles of humanism

> form a narrow catwalk without railings that must, by obli-
> gation, be crossed while pretending that one feels neither
> fear nor vertigo. Advancing in life, fists clenched, eyes ter-
> ribly knowledgeable, and vibrant with identity.

Once again the image of walking is striking, linked this time to fear and vertigo that must not be shown. On the contrary, we must "advance in life, fists clenched," looking "vibrant with identity." In this poetic writing, the contamination between "clenched" and "identity" is not the result of chance. For the narrator rejects the vision of an identity enclosed in fine humanitarian principles that make it impossible to "réfléchir adéquatement sur le sens de la vie" ["reflect adequate-ly on the meaning of life" (71)]. What she seeks is an identity that leaves room for unspoken questioning, making it possible to situate oneself outside of received discourses. She finds this room in fiction: "Peut-on sor-tir de l'humanité sans entrer dans la fiction?" ["Is it possible to move outside humanity without entering fiction?" (72)].

An author's work develops in coherent ways. Nicole Brossard is pursuing here a reflection begun in the 1980s in which she has insisted upon the need for fiction in order to remove oneself from reality, especial-ly so in the case of women. This was well developed in *The Aerial Letter*, particularly "Access to Writing: Rites of Language" (131-139, 139-147). In the novel *Hier*, for example, the female characters continue to try to open for themselves a mental space suitable for new thought.

What is more, the last chapter of the novel begins with writing notes that the narrator has made trying to "comprendre ce qui était arrivé mais sans chercher à tirer une conclusion" ["understand what had happened but without trying to draw a conclusion" (336)]. Through writing, the narrator is trying to do the work of vigilant watching. In this vein, the novel ends with the following words: "Tant mieux si l'écriture permet de détourner le cours des choses et d'irriguer là où le coeur est sec et demandant." And as if she were aware of the fact that this is a dream, she adds in a new paragraph: "C'est juste une petite phrase pour guérir" ["So much the better if writing allows for a shift in the course of things, a watering there where the heart is parched and demanding. It is just one small sentence for healing" (346, trans. Karen McPherson)].

The circle is complete. She who in the opening lines of the novel was "trying to preserve," to commit to writing "the memory of landscapes," leaves notes "dans l'espoir que rien de ce qui fut n'ait été inutile" ["in the hope that nothing of what was has been useless" (336)]. It is impossible not to see that Nicole Brossard's ethical vision has evolved since the 1970s, the era when great ideologies prevailed: one no longer writes today with the pretension of radically changing the world. One limits oneself to the wish of being witness to one's time, with the hope that fiction will end up having an influence on reality. That it will have a healing effect …On oneself, on others, on humanity?

In the text, the verb "healing" has no object. Its interpretation remains open.

Witness of the World

Giving witness to the world: this desire appears to me to take into account the initiative taken by all Québec novelist-poets, who do not write to add stories to the many stories which encumber bookstores, but to commit life's movement to writing, to ensure that fiction reveals a part of what is real but concealed, to serve women as speech on which they can depend. The narrator of *Hier* says: "Toutes les filles rêvent d'une mère qui pourrait leur apprendre le monde, la réalité et en même temps les faire rêver" ["All girls dream of a mother who could teach them the world, reality, and at the same time make them dream" (293-294)]. The space of fiction thus makes itself the space of transmission. As in *These Our Mothers*, novelists become symbolic mothers, to use Brossard's expression, mothers who are not content to reproduce the values of the Fathers, but claim to be their own value producers. They seek to commit cultural memory *au féminin* to writing for their daughters, making it possible for them to develop their own reading of the world – in the final analysis, to bring healing from the "silence ingouvernable" ["ungovernable silence" (346)] constituted by civilization's millennial memory.

According to Jean-Yves Tadié "les récits poétiques

de notre temps veulent rendre compte du sens du monde par des systèmes de symboles" ["Poetic narratives of our times attempt to report on the meaning of the world through systems of symbols" (145)]. The same didactic dimension characterizing mythological texts is evident here: the text seeks less to represent a specific situation – social, political or individual – than to develop models from it which derive a sacred value by serving as a reference point, a learning opportunity. The novel *Hier* is certainly in this current, since it proposes a revised and corrected version of the world through unveiling a memory of the past inscribed in the present with the objective of preparing the future. This is a memory that can come only from an attitude of resistance to received values, allied with an immense desire for creation in language, because, as the narrative voice says in *Langues obscures*, "écrire n'a de sens que pour s'appliquer à bien vivre" ["writing's only meaning is to apply oneself for living well" (28)]. For Nicole Brossard, the word *Life* is at the same time the word at the end and at the beginning.

Notes

1. This is a translation of a conference paper, "Le roman des frontières," given in 2002 by Louise Dupré. It has since been published with minor modifications as "Le roman des frontières," *Aux frontières des deux genres: en hommage à Andrée Chedid*, 131-143. Translation of the original conference paper and other citations are by LHF, unless otherwise indicated.

2. In this regard see Hector de Saint-Denys Garneau, "Accompagnement" (34), Gaston Miron, "La Marche à l'amour" (33-46), France Théoret, "La Marche" (23-34).

3. This is a famous line from French poet Arthur Rimbaud – translator's note.

Works Cited

Buci-Glucksmann, Christine. *La raison baroque: de Baudelaire à Benjamin*. Paris: Galilée, 1984.

Combe, Dominique. "La référence dédoublée: le sujet lyrique entre fiction et autobiographie." *Figures du sujet lyrique*. Ed. Dominique Rabaté. Paris: Presses Universitaires de France. 1996. Coll. "Perspectives littéraires. 39-63.

Dupré, Louise. *Stratégies du vertige. Trois poètes: Nicole Brossard, Madeleine Gagnon, France Théoret*. Montréal: Éditions du Remue-Ménage, 1989.

——. "Le roman des frontières." *Aux frontières des deux genres: En hommage à Andrée Chedid*. Ed. Carmen Boustani. Paris: Karthala, 2003. 131-43

Garneau, Hector de Saint-Denys. *Regards et jeux dans l'espace. Oeuvres*. Ed. Jacques Brault and Benoît Lacroix. Montréal: Les Presses de l'Université de Montréal, 1971.

Gaudet, Gérald. "Liminaire," "La Séduction du romanesque," *Estuaire*. 37 (1985): 7.

Miron, Gaston. *L'homme rapaillé*. Montréal: Les Presses de l'Université de Montréal, 1970.

Tadié, Jean-Yves. *Le récit poétique*. Paris: Gallimard, 1994. Coll. "Tel."

Théoret, France. *Nécessairement putain*. Montréal: Les Herbes rouges, 1980.

Flirting with the Museum Narrative

From Picture Theory *to* Hier

CLAUDINE POTVIN

Considering the text as a museum narrative, I will examine here the relation between the literary and the visual arts in Nicole Brossard's writing. In this context, a brief commentary on *Picture Theory, Mauve Desert, Baroque at Dawn* will serve as an introduction to *Hier*, Brossard's last novel. In these novels, rather than a simple illustration or a gloss, the work of art is inscribed as structural element or principle of composition of the text. In what I consider to be a text-museum, the art object finds itself as part of the narrative through the narrator, a character, a series of motifs, or is described/located within the story as a reference, a form of explanation, a meaning. This is to say that I situate myself in a verbal order, in the *ekfrasis*, since the mention of, or allusion to, the visual has primarily a narrative function. The interpretation of a specific image (real or imaginary), present in or suggested by the text, as well as of the creative process, is determined essentially by the narrator's voice and gaze. As the fiction becomes a translation of art into words, the image signifies through written language. Thus, to read a story through and with the image supposes a certain contemplation of forms, shapes, colours evoked between the lines.

As feminist critics have argued in recent decades, visual forms underlying fiction (painting, photograph, frame, bodies, museum, installation, exhibition, etc.) can be effective in questioning the politics as well as the semantics and the aesthetics of the *official* gaze that has viewed and evaluated women and art through history. In that sense, Brossard explores in her fictions a museographic experience as a new form of rapport between the reader/spectator/*voyeur* and the text. My study of this particular aspect of Brossard's narrative strategies shows that the visual, the *image*, permeates her writings in order to establish the link between a given visual aesthetics, some literary practices and a contemporary feminist epistemology. Since my analysis is not centered on the image or illustration *per se* but rather metaphorically, I will consider its textual significance as a function of the processes of production and reception themselves which generate the text through a multiplicity of optical arrangements. The word *illustration*, which meant in old French *apparition*, signals the image's purpose in the text. According to Hubert Damish an illustration provides visual representation for something that would normally be difficult to envisage: "il s'agit, dans tous les cas, de donner à voir, de manifester sous une espèce concrète, un objet, un phénonène, un événement, une pensée qui, dans les conditions normales d'appréhension ou de lecture, échapperait à toute prise sensible, au moins immédiate" (7).

In many ways, Nicole Brossard's writings belong to a museum culture as they recreate a *museum* or *tableau* effect, not only because a certain image (or an allusion to one) strikes the reader or because a form of art is inscribed within the text as a reference or a writing process, but equally because her fictions tend to deconstruct the very system of representation that defines them. In parallel, the book/museum reduces the border between presentation and representation, reproduction and myth. Ultimately, this essay explores how the museum constitutes one of the visual scenes that characterize Brossard's writings as well as how her texts transform themselves into museum.

Object, commentary, description, fiction by turns, the image belongs to or is part of the story, the same way that the word frames the picture. In this context, the terms museum, art, painting, canvas, ruins (in an archeological perspective), frames, are to be seen here in a broad sense, as writing and art include each other. In *Travaux sémiotiques*, Nycole Paquin refers to a *corps-à-corps* in these terms: "Déjà répertorié, attribué, historicisé et monumentalisé, le tableau [that is the museum and/or the text as museum] sera entendu comme programme ouvert, c'est-à-dire comme matrice à laquelle tout récepteur se prend en vertu d'un savoir qui lui est propre et qu'il rend au système double du support: image et texte" (97). The museum is, by

extension, an open space, an architectural and ideological construct: building or monument geographically
circumscribed, conceived, imagined and produced, fiction, metafiction, always infinite in its articulations and
meanings. The museum, whether institution or literary representation, maintains a socio-cultural discourse on all art forms located in its walls and, conse-
quently, on the reader. The museum's context is never
given or natural but produced since it implies a process
of selection of the chosen collections, the order of
which recreates an illusion of coherence or logic, even
value. As Douglas Crimp writes, the postmodern
museum is simultaneously a space of exclusion and
confinement (1987: 62).

Foucault considers the museum as one of Western
culture's privileged heterotopias (concrete or realized
utopia), along with the library, the university, the road,
the garden and other spaces. The heterotopia, like the
utopia, is a "*non-lieu*," that is a *here* and *nowhere*.
When Northrop Frye asks where is Utopia, he answers
"nowhere," which is the same as "here." According to
Frye, these new utopias/heterotopias "would be rooted
in the body as well as in the mind, in the unconscious
as well as in the conscious, in forests and deserts as well
as in highways and buildings, in bed as in the symposium" (49). The museum provides, possibly better than
any other space, an instance of the fixity of that which
is exposed on the one hand, as much as the limits of the
viewer's past and present possibilities on the other. In

general, one visits a museum with one of two attitudes: either static, vertical, and ritual, or else dynamic and dialogic. Whether the visitor knows it or not, a set of semiotic codes more or less identified serve as orientation markers in this utopian country. When Brossard articulates her text around artistic principles and when her characters engage in a ludic/reading activity, she is obviously rethinking art and literature, engaging with the art object in a dynamic conversation and a productive dialogue. Brossard refuses the ritual attitude absolutely; on the contrary, she establishes a circulation principle, a spiral (dear to the author), a rhizomatic position, a manner of looking that denies fixity.

As border, reflection, projection, the museum permeates Brossard's writings as a historical and political *monument*, private and public. Archeology and aesthetics, the text/museum constitutes the frame that allows the inscription of knowledge outside canonical discourse, outside patriarchy. Sexual/textual phantasm, intimate or collective, women's *parole* leaves traces on the body of Art and History.[1]

What I am calling the museum here is present in many of Brossard's novels: from *Picture Theory*, *Mauve Desert* to *Baroque at dawn*, the author has explored through the museum experience the screen, the urban scene, the black and white photographs of *l'homme long*, the beauty of a woman called La Sixtine as in the Sistine Chapel, the allure of civilization. In these novels, women circulate in writing as in museums, deconstructing and rethinking the narrative, as well as historical and literary models. The museological image brings into sight a certain concept of the beautiful and the civilized, which throws into question traditional aesthetic figures and includes a trajectory, a view of sexuality, and a way of thinking in the feminine.

In *Picture Theory*, there are only five mentions of the museum and a few artistic allusions (*tableau*, *toile*, *stèle*). The museum experience is nonetheless determined entirely by the character's desire, that of the woman who walks and "entre au Musée" (*PT* 45, 46, 56). The museum becomes experimental space for the narrator, who installs herself and her practice in the museum room and examines a women's body. The perception of the museum and of some objects exposed there reflects the theory contained in the book's title: a *picture*, a screen, a painting, a scene that serve to project the narrator's story (reproductions, copies, frames, captured and subverted from institutional discourse). As the narrator moves in and out of the museum, the art of writing on and looking at skins or textures takes on a life of its own, outside of walls, as in Beaubourg:

> L'éclat du musée. Mille fragments retombent sur mes épaules. De la matière partout, pièces d'identité: notes, lipstick, miroir, condom, clés, argent, mille fragments s'assemblent sous nos yeux dans le musée, dans le livre, il faut les voir venir (*PT*f 130).

Shattering of the museum. Thousands of fragments fall
upon my shoulders. Material everywhere, pièces d'identité:
notes, lipstick, mirror, condom, keys, money, a thousand
fragments gather under your eyes in the museum, in the
book, you must see them coming (*PT*e 106).

The book becomes museum; the book is the exhibition, the illustration, the extension of the gallery, the
imaginary territory where the women's *continent*
acquires a form of reality.[2] The five studious and radical women of *Picture Theory* inhabit the museum's
spaces as a technique to rethink abstraction, language,
and the art of leaving; the museum manifests itself as
limit, allegory, décor, frame, exchange, introspection,
gaze.

Photographs linked to Longman have a definite aesthetic function in *Mauve Desert,* mathematical logic
being disturbed by the progressive blurring overtone of
reality. However, it is in the body of the text and the
translation operation that Brossard intercepts this reality and disrupts the coherence of expressions of civilization. The first narrator (Laure Angstelle) creates new
utopias through a reflexive process. The second narrator (Maude Laures), who interrogates the originality
and the authenticity of an original text, installs her own
writing as original. To work on a translation is to imagine how a painting transforms the painter's perception
into lines and meaning. The concrete world (motel,
pool, car, T.V., tattoo, revolver, bar), the photographic
plates, the cinematographic background (desert, dawn,

light, beauty, fear, etc.) construct boundaries between reality and fiction and authorize the passage of a type of narrative to another. Maude dreams that one day it will be possible to translate or erase the disturbing bodies that impede perception of literature's beauty as reproduced on the walls of Amargosa Opera as Spanish figures from the seventeenth century. In the first row, "des femmes qui chuchotent, un mouchoir, un éventail à la main. Le rouge et le bleu des robes, poitrines toute chair, d'étranges coiffes, tout cela qui forme une civilisation quand on regarde au fond des yeux l'expression"(*DM* 100) ["women whispering, a handkerchief, a fan in their hand. The red and blue of the dresses, bosoms all of flesh, strange headdresses, everything that shapes a civilization when one looks at the expression deeply in the eyes" (*MD* 93)]. Facing the picture, Angela Parkins wonders if it was not "l'expression du regard qui permettait de distinguer parmi les outils, les armes et les ornements, comment la mort pouvait être vaincue, comment les femmes, esclaves parmi les esclaves, pouvaient s'adonner dans leur forme arrondie à la vie?" (*DM* 100) ["the expression in the gaze that made it possible to distinguish between the tools, the weapons and the ornaments, how death can be vanquished, how women, slaves among slaves, could in their rounded form be party to life?" (*MD* 93-94)]. At that point, the writer/translator questions precisely, as viewer, all interpretations suggested by the received perspective on things (esthetic, literary, historical).

The same observation can be made regarding La Sixtine's character in *Baroque d'aube*. In response to her objection that she is not sixteen, Cybil Noland, her lover, answers calling her La Sixtine. The first part of the novel, "Hôtel Rafale," develops piece by piece, line by line, the portrait of a beautiful girl, young, musician, passionate: "La plupart du temps, le visage dessinait sa propre aura d'extase à partir de la lumière filtrant par la fente énigmatique que forment les paupières quand elles restent entrouvertes à égale distance de la vie et du plaisir" (*BA* 19) ["Most often the face would describe its own aura of ecstasy, beginning with the light filtering through the enigmatic slit between the eyelids when they hover half-closed halfway between life and pleasure" (*BD* 12)]. The portrait defines an art of *jouissance* as much as the pleasure of the artist who recognizes in the features of the young woman the happiness of invention. Obviously, I am not referring here to a portrait sketched by a skilful artist in search of a pseudo-resemblance nor to a detailed description, but to the construction of a woman/artist recreated through a series of abstractions. After all, La Sixtine composes her performer's face. She

> manie habilement les éponges, les crayons et les pinceaux pour qu'ils sécrètent fard, poudre, mascara comme des matières à spectacle capables d'assombrir le jour et d'éclairer le sentiment, couleurs qu'on insère dans le rêve pour y faire briller la nuit (*BA* 41-2).

deftly wields her pads, pencils and brushes, makes them
secrete the makeup, the powder, mascara and so on, show-
biz props capable of darkening the day and brightening
feelings, colours that one inserts in a dream to make the
night resplendent (*BD* 34).

Paula Rea Radisich argues that "the self-portrait offers
its maker a degree of control over self-representation"
(445). In the same way, the text tends to perform as a
possible museum capable of generating images whereby the museum assumes control over its own representation.

Although in a different register, Brossard's last
novel, *Hier* exemplifies this construction of a representational system through words and images. The museum (edifice, institution, exhibition) constitutes the
central paradigm of the novel. *Hier* contains five parts.
The first one, equally named "Hier," is composed of
seventy-nine brief fragments which form a *tableau* in
which four women united by work, family, pleasure,
and circumstances, question the meaning of civilization and death. This is a quartette that Hélène Rioux
describes as a "ballet de voix" (19). Four exemplary
women: Simone Lambert, curator at the Museum of
Civilization in Quebec City; Axelle, her granddaughter, geneticist; the writer Carla Carlson from Saskatoon
who revives through her Swedish mother and her
imagination the death of Descartes and who always
comes to complete her novels in Quebec City; the narrator, Simone's assistant and Carla's confidant. In an

apparently transparent mode, Brossard very often begins the narration of various fragments with the word *hier*. Occasionally, she integrates the adverb into the middle of the segment or towards the end, erasing the definite irreversibility of the time category. Interwoven throughout the text is a page, an *aquarelle [water colour]*, an illustration of a love scene lost in words and future:

> Des mots sont là que je n'arrive pas à bien distinguer, se*i*ns, *vent*re, bl*h*anche, s*t*exe et entre eux, les lèvres de la femme remuent comme une eau de vie qui lave de tout cliché, promet que chaque empreinte du regard sera sexuelle sera répétée et fluide aussi vive que la lumière du matin qui absorbe les pensées les plus intimes […] le regard de la femme s'engouffre dans le futur (*H* 49).

> There are words which I can't make out very well, *se*i*ns, *ventre*, bl*h*anche, s*t*exe* and between them, the woman's lips stir like an *eau de vie* that cleanses from all clichés, promises that every imprint of the look will be sexual will be repeated and fluid as lively as the morning light which absorbs the most intimate thoughts [...] the woman's look throws itself into the gulf of the future. [3]

The sequence will indeed be repeated five times without change, although visualizing/reading the same scene/image supposes a look constantly modified through time and space. The graphic game accentuates the visualization phenomenon.

In the second section, *Les urnes [The Urns]*, the reader accompanies Simone Lambert, as she (re)visits her exhibition. From the other side of the mirror, as she assumes the role of spectator, Simone contemplates the urns which have survived through centuries. We learn later that *Siècles lointains [Distant Centuries]*, name given by Simone to her exhibition, "ne semblait plus s'appliquer au passé mais bel et bien au futur" ["no longer seemed to apply to the past but quite nicely to the future" (*H* 212)]. The following mental and physical representations in the mind and life of Simone, a form of animated art, belong in effect to the future; they expose what is already there, what is already spoken or written. They are the very representation of the necessity to create a repertory of gestures and words suggested by this remark made by the narrator: "je collectionne des images de ruines, des angles morts de civilisation. Je m'entoure de débris, des reliquats de splendeurs anciennes, de vieux précis de composition" ["I am a collector of images of ruins, of civilization's dead angles. I surround myself with debris, with the remains of ancient splendours, with old composition precis" (*H* 266)].

"Yesterday" is intimately linked to the present in this novel, despite the fact that each one of the four women involved in her personal past reality, her own crypt or drama, exists almost outside of the temporal dimension, be it through travel, memory as a movement more than an incident recalled, invention, recreation of a theatre without development, death. The anonymous narrator, Simone's assistant, prepares for herself an exhibition on ruins. She thinks that "Les ruines contemporaines sont à nos pensées ce que la corrosion est aux matières premières, elles déposent en nous des images d'abandon qui contaminent à tout jamais notre sens de la durée" ["Contemporary ruins are to our thoughts what corrosion is to primary matter. They deposit images of abandonment in us which contaminate for all time our sense of enduring" (128)].

Ruin, mausoleum, the museum suggests the existence of objects totally disconnected from their context or from a present that would apparently justify their existence. Protected, hanging on the wall, installed under the light of memories, the work of art recreates for the museum's visitor a sensation of vacuum that leaves nonetheless traces in the form of emotions. This applies even for the museum curator:

> Lundi soir, le musée est fermé. Simone déambule dans la grande salle d'exposition où le silence et la solitude forment un couple invitant. [...] Au mai de lilas et au bleu versatile du fleuve, elle préfère la parenthèse temporelle, la chute dans le temps que représente *Siècles lointains* (*H* 201).

> Monday evening, the museum is closed. Simone meanders in the large exhibition hall where silence and solitude form an inviting couple. [...] To the May of lilacs and the versatile blue of the river, she prefers the temporal parenthesis, the collapse into time that *Distant Centuries* represents.

Archeologist by profession, Simone has spent years excavating her own past from ancient sites; she has searched among sacred bodies for the meaning of death. Here, death appears as a continuum that establishes the novel's characters within the silence of civilizations. Simone has lost her lover Alice on the eve of one of these expeditions; she is now waiting for her granddaughter, whose mother has disappeared; every day, the narrator, driven herself by her mother's death, meets the writer Carla Carlson at the Hotel Clarendon. She needs Carlson, who remembers her father's story, in order to relive the death of Descartes. In the middle of these *revelations*, Brossard introduces the sudden death of Fabrice Lacoste, close colleague at the Museum: one more absence, one final fade out, an avoidable yesterday.

Quoting Adorno ("*Valéry Proust Museum*"), Douglas Crimp noted in his article "On the Museum's Ruins": "The German word *museal* (museumlike) has unpleasant overtones. It describes objects to which the observer no longer has a vital relationship and which are in the process of dying. They owe their preservation more to historical respect than to the needs of the present. Museum and mausoleum are connected by more than phonetic association. Museums are like the family sepulchres of works of art" (1980: 41). In *Hier*, the word death resorbs itself into the present of the show and lesbian desire. Brossard displaces Adorno's discourse, since she understands civilization outside of the classical canon. In that sense, *hier* could be, is, today, now, soon, tomorrow, the day/century before.

Death appears each time closer to life. It is one among many of life's figures. Each death has to be exposed, recuperated, translated in a dialogue, a play, characterized by the lack of conflict, a strange form of eroticism. No action then, no destiny, no confrontation; hardly a reality elaborated in a true bar, in a room decorated for the circumstance with the notes of a writer who delivers her text at an impressive velocity. The narrator states that we are watching a women's theatre, the same way we used to talk about *l'écriture au féminin,* as she stresses that we, the spectators, cannot expect this theatre to be as action-filled and lively as usual:

> Le fait qu'aucun élement générateur de conflit (compétition, antagonisme, désaccord) n'intervienne entre les femmes rend particulièrement difficile l'inscription de moments d'extrême tension, voire même de violence verbale dont le theâtre est en général tributaire. En effet, pas de couple, pas de lien viscéral ou passionnel. Pas de jalousie, de haine, d'amour. Pas d'intimité, pas de quotidien entre les personnages (*H* 219).

> The fact that no element generating conflict (competition, antagonism, disagreement) intervenes between the women makes particularly difficult the inscription of moments of extreme tension, indeed even of verbal violence, upon which the theatre generally depends. In effect, there is no couple, no visceral or passionate bond. No jealousy, no hatred, no love. No intimacy, no quotidian between the characters.

In this dialogue, the four women are listened to, looked at, perceived, admired as *masterpieces* winking at the passersby, watching for a reaction while the others observe. Similarly, if the objects could talk to each other in a gallery or a museum, they would not risk pulling each other's hair since they appear fixed, static, many times closed upon themselves, silent, even thought they are entirely open to the art-lover's gaze.

In the third and fourth parts of her novel, respectively *Hôtel Clarendon* and *La chambre de Carla Carlson [Carla Carlson's room]*, Brossard develops eight visual scenes: a reading of Carla's text and a dialogue, in which the representation of the drama becomes movement or screen through the power of language. The verbal exchanges among the four women situated partly in an unknown territory place the reader/viewer in a position of interpreter as we approach the painting or the urn in order to decipher the information given in the margin of the frame (generally the name of the artist, title, date, a few details, etc.). However, Brossard always resists the temptation of the description. First of all, the author situates her characters in a not so canonical museum making clear that any "museum of civilization" could represent a bridge between old and new, past and future, ancient worlds and colonies, sacred art and daily perspective, death and life. Furthermore, one of the functions of the museum is certainly to collect, conserve, protect the artifacts that are judged worthy of exposition and interest. The narrator collects moments, visual impressions, scenes, emotions:

> Toujours faire semblant d'être du côté de la vraie vie. Journée d'éclairs et d'électricité foudroyante. J'accumule les notes, les pensées sur les ruines, le passé. Hier, un autre terrible orage. Pendant ma visite au musée, nous avons manqué d'électricité (*H* 341).

> Always pretend to be on the side of real life. Day of lightning bolts and thundering electricity. I accumulate notes, thoughts on ruins, the past. Yesterday, another terrible storm. During my visit to the museum we were without electricity.

In his work *Posibilidades y límites de comunicación museográfica*, Lauro Zavala defines the museum as a space of excess. In the museum, one finds the social excess of information as well as the personal excess of time; in the museum, argues Zavala, the existence of exposed objects becomes also excessive in utilitarian terms. Eccentric and asymmetric, the museological discourse appropriates the multiple spaces of the street, history, culture, art, subjectivity, etc., closing or opening the perspectives and possibilities of literature, equally a site of excess, surplus, pleasure, for no reason at all.

Brossard's novel is also a space of excess since there is always a surplus of words and meanings that readers must deal with. In the museum's world, excess is a form as much as a meaning, an attitude contained already in the notion of frame. In derridian terms, the *parergon* (*cadre*/frame) "vient contre, à côté et en plus de l'*ergon*, du travail fait, du fait, de l'œuvre mais il ne tombe pas à côté, il touche et coopère, depuis un certain dehors, simplement dedans. Comme un accessoire qu'on est obligé d'acceuillir au bord, à bord. Il est d'abord l'à-bord" (63). As accessory, the frame invites the reader to come inside, to come and look.

Brossard has always subverted all frames in her writings (syntax, grammar, chronology, linearity, gender, genre, etc.). In *Hier,* more than transgressing the idea of the frame seen as an object that surrounds the "main picture" or a so-called central story, she integrates it and transforms its function. Visually and literally speaking, frame refers to edge, container, box, limit, extremity, margin, but is equally *clin* d'oeil, allusion, invitation, part. In reality, rather than erasing the frame, Brossard displaces it. In the novel, the book itself, the narrative, the characters, the chapters, the museums, become both framed and framing elements. The frame, signifier and signified, not only adds or encloses but also blends with the image. What matters in Brossard's novel is the fact that the whole book seems to be framing a story (within a story), working as a frame that matters not only to accompany but to indicate the importance of the envelope (the exhibition, the window, the glass, the play, the bar, the room, the city, the river, the page, etc.).

The various mentions of artists in the novel (Krieghoff, Frida Kahlo, Titian, Magritte, Caravaggio, Pannini, Velasquez, Millet, Jordi Bonet, etc., to name only a few), form a visual or virtual library that integrates the inscription of Art within the text, but above all submits the artistic lens and the *voyeur*'s gaze to the test of daily experience, particularly that of four women with a passion for words and images. Simone's granddaughter, Axelle, represents the one (the *"elle"*) who will cut the world/words with an "ax", in order to rearrange it and to design the future. After all, she has been cut herself from her past; she has been separated from her lineage, she has been removed from her place of origin. It is not by chance that she works in genetics, science of heredity or manipulation and mutation of genes.

By giving to her novel the title *Hier*, Nicole Brossard fabricates from the very beginning a false trail, a deceptive background; she suggests a lasting vision reinforced within the concept of masterpieces. To frequent works of art, as proposed by the narrator and the characters, is to understand or to read as a process of annotation, writing, skimming through, caressing, a process closely associated with the desire of a woman for another woman. In the fifth and final chapter, the narrator confesses:

> J'ai pris des notes jusqu'à la fin sans m'apercevoir que la fin était arrivée. Je voulais que chaque instant soit entier, que rien ne m'échappe de la chambre ni du décor. Du visage ni des masques. J'ai noté attentivement la disposition

du corps, la place des meubles, la lumière du dehors et l'é-
clairage du dedans (*H* 329).

I took notes right to the end without noticing that the end
had arrived. I wanted for every instant to be complete, for
nothing to escape me about the room or the *décor*. About
the face or the masks. I took attentive note of the disposi-
tion of the body, the place of the furniture, the light from
the outside and the inside lighting.

Somebody will find these "Quelques notes trouvées
dans la chambre de l'Hôtel Clarendon" ["Few notes
found in the room at the Hôtel Clarendon" (*H* 337-
346)] addendum to an already annotated story by
which no final meaning can be presumed.

Interestingly enough, Simone's assistant just signed
a contract with a community Maison de Culture from
Montréal for an exhibition on *Migrants et Gitans*. The
literary and the visual mutate and the brossardian
museum proposes multiple associations of words and
images. Representation is always displaced as the refer-
ent ceases to signify in the context of ancient civilizations only. Words and images are never in an absolute
position of reflection; it is rather a question of tongues
and languages, bodies and minds, elasticity and reach.
It is a matter of stretching memory. Finally, "La
mémoire, on dit que c'est du silence ingouvernable.
Tant mieux si l'écriture permet de détourner le cours
des choses et d'irriguer là où le cœur est sec et demandant" ["Memory, they say it's ungovernable silence. So
much the better if writing makes it possible to alter the

course of things and to provide irrigation there where the heart is dry and demanding" (*H* 346)].

Hier exemplifies how Brossard opens, from a textual and discursive point of view, the traditionally closed space of the museum, often located in restricted buildings, to dialogue, mutation and circulation. From masterpiece to popular artifact, from excavation to exhibition, from dogmas to sexualities, art moves beautifully under Nicole Brossard's pen.

Notes

1. Eugenio Donato, who studied the representation of museums in Flaubert *(Bouvard et Pécuchet)*, refers to an archeological concept of origin: "Its representational and historical pretensions are based upon a number of metaphysical assumptions about origins. Archeology intends, after all, to be a science of the arches" (220).

2. I am grateful to Louise Forsyth for having drawn my attention to the cover of the English translation of *Picture Theory*. The museum motif appears there in the illustration of Athena reproduced on a Greek pitcher dating from 430 before the modern era. The reference to Antiquity, as well as the energy and the movement of the figure, functions to frame the feminine body of the studious women of *Picture Theory*, who are thereby projected toward a spatial and dynamic utopia, in much the same way as the museal forms of *Hier*.

3. All translations from *Hier* are by LHF.

Works Cited

Crimp, Douglas. "On the Museum's Ruins." *October*. 13 (1980): 41-57.

Crimp, Douglas. "The Postmodern Museum." *Parachute* (March-May 1987): 61-69.

Damisch, Hubert. "La peinture prise au mot." *Les Mots et les Images*. Préface. Meyer Schapiro. Paris : Macula, 2000. 5-27.

Derrida, Jacques. *La vérité en peinture*. Paris: Flammarion, 1978.

Donato, Eugenio. "The Museum's Furnace: Notes Toward a Contextual Reading of *Bouvard and Pécuchet*." *Textual Strategies: Perspectives in Post-Structuralist Criticism*. Ithaca: Cornell University Press, 1979. 215-232.

Foucault, Michel. "Des espaces autres." *Dits et écrits*. Paris: Gallimard, 1994. 752-62.

Frye, Northrop. "Varieties of Literary Utopias." *Utopias and Utopian Thought*. Ed. F.E. Manuel. Boston: Houghton Mifflin Company, 1966. 47-65.

Paquin, Nycole. "Corps à corps: l'objet d'art et son récepteur." *Travaux sémiotiques*. Ed.

Jacques Allard. Montréal: Les Cahiers du département d'études littéraires, UQAM, 1984. 97- 118.

Radisich, Paula Rea. "Qui peut définir les femmes? Vigée-Lebrun's Portraits of an Artist." *Eighteenth-Century Studies*. 25. 4 (Summer 1992): 441-67.

Rioux, Hélène. "Terra incognita." *Lettres québécoises*. 106 (été 2002): 19-20.

Zavala, Lauro, Ma de la Paz Silva and Francisco Villasenor. *Posibilidades y límites de la comunicación museográfica*. México: Universidad Nacional Autónoma de México, 1993.

Moving into the Third Dimension

Nicole Brossard's Picture Theory

KATHARINE CONLEY

Beginning with the title reference to Ludwig
Wittgenstein's *Tractatus Logico-Philosophicus*, Nicole
Brossard incorporates familiar textual voices into
Picture Theory, her densely polyphonic novel from
1982, and thickens it with cross references, casting
shadows within it. The novel's intertexts are lit by
Brossard's vision of the hologram as a model for writing as articulated in her essay "The Aerial Letter" from
1980, rather than by Cartesian patriarchal reason. The
intellectual space of the novel drifts, according to
Picture Theory's emblematic word (and name) *dérive*
(Dérive), or turns around the reader like a translucent
textual scarf, leaving the impression of having traversed
a geographic space in which overlapping realities coexist. With *Picture Theory*, Brossard moves into the
third dimension of writing and seals her poetic francophone feminist vision.[1]

In "The Aerial Letter" Brossard advocates "une
nouvelle écriture: de dérive. Peut-être alors faire preuve
d'imagination en ouvrant une brèche: spirale" (*LA* 50)
["a new writing: one that drifts, that slips out from
under; writing that eludes. Why not then submit proof

of imagination by opening a breach: a spiral?" (*AL* 72)]. One way Brossard enacts this "spiral" strategy is through the recasting of well-known literary and philosophical texts. Evoking Pascal's injunction to consider the imponderability of the heart (which has reasons of which reason knows nothing), for instance, Brossard declares: "car le corps a ses raisons" (*LA* 51) ["For the body has its reasons" (*AL* 74)], thus rereading and concretizing Pascal's conceptual heart. In a repositioning of one of Stéphane Mallarmé's most famous titles she links chance to the writing body and texts to habitable space:

> Mais qui sont ces femmes qui me donnent du texte à penser, de l'espace à conquérir [...]? Je les appelle urbaines radicales. Le hasard, du genre de celui qu'aucun coup de dé n'abolira, veut qu'elles soient lesbiennes de peau et d'écriture (*LA* 58).

> But who are these women who give me texts which make me think, a space I can take over and inhabit [...]? I call them urban radicals. Chance, the kind no throw of the dice will ever abolish, has it that they are lesbians, by their skin and by their writing (*AL* 80).

Her focus on spatialisation culminates in her aerial vision:

> La lettre aérienne, c'est le fantasme qui me donne à lire et à écrire en trois dimensions, c'est mon laser. Espace-temps-mobilité dans l'Histoire [...] voir l'Histoire à même sa peau (*LA* 65-6).

The aerial letter is the fantasy which permits me to read and write in three dimensions; it is my laser. Space-time-mobility in History [...] seeing History right down to the skin (*AL* 86).

In *Picture Theory* Brossard turns to Wittgenstein's proposition from the *Tractus* that "The picture is a model of reality" (39). With the understanding that "one can not express reality, one can only show it [sic]," Brossard causes language to make "pictures" with white space, italics, and typography, as well as with her evocation of the hologram (Cotnoir 122). She responds implicitly to Wittgenstein's questioning of Descartes's *cogito* and explores explicitly his idea of language as a tool, from the *Philosophical Investigations*, whereby how a word is used counts as much as what it stands for.[2] For example, with the name Claire Dérive from *Picture Theory*, Brossard plays both functions off one another, so that they shed light on each other, because its "use" as a proper name is haunted by what it "stands for," Clear Drift. Literally *clear* and not opaque, like most unfamiliar fictional names, Claire Dérive's name announces Brossard's intention to write in a manner "that is both *derived from* and *adrift*," as Karen Gould suggests, and to embody this writing in a fictional desiring and desirable woman's body (88). Brossard's style as well recalls Wittgenstein's, who has been characterized as "the most radical of modernist writers" by Marjorie Perloff, "a writer for whom any totalizing scheme must always give way to 'travel over a wide field of thought criss-cross in every direction.' Only such criss-cross advances our thinking" (66).

Picture Theory "criss-crosses" in several ways beginning with its structure: complementary first and last sections flank two tripartite middle sections. The book's first section, "L'ordinaire" ["The Ordinary"], proposes through its title that which is quotidian and iterative as non- chronological, non-linear elements of Brossard's "picture theory." Brossard encourages the reader to follow a reading process that itself approximates non-linearity – implicitly with multiple cross references and explicitly by sending the reader to page 162 from page 34 and back again and to page 149 [sic] from page 115 (pages 185, 40, 167in French text). "The Ordinary" introduces the narrator, Michèle Vallée, her lover, Claire Dérive, and Claire's family, with poetic simultaneity. Succeeding paragraphs situate the characters in diverse spaces – Montreal, Paris, New York, together with Curaçao and Ogunquit – as they think about or communicate with one another long distance. Even apart in space, in transit, they are often together in time, just as Claire's voice on Michèle's answering machine, spoken in the past, articulates the phrase "*Je suis Claire Dérive*" in the present tense, and thus conjures her absent presence and prompts time periods to overlap (*PT*f42, *PT*e36).

The first paragraph opens in the bar of a hotel on Curaçao where the narrator has met a woman named Anna by chance and where she (the narration's "I") is addressed as "you" by a dancer whose comment identifies one of the key elements in a hologram: that every part contains the whole:

> Dans le bar du Hilton, le danseur des Caraïbes dit: vous vous souviendrez sans doute de Curaçao à cause d'un détail (Anna, que le hasard m'avait fait rencontrer quelques heures auparavant, m'avait prévenue qu'une réalité n'en recouvre pas nécessairement une autre mais qu'hôtesse de l'air entre le Venezuela et Aruba la laissait à désirer) (*PT*f 19).

> In the bar of the Hilton, the dancer from the Caribbean says: you will undoubtedly remember Curaçao because of a detail (Anna, whom I had met by chance a few hours earlier, had warned me that one reality did not necessarily overlap another but air stewardess between Venezuela and Aruba left her to desire) (*PT*e 15).

With this first sentence the reader is plunged into a dialogue in the present between a woman and a man under which, parenthetically, the remembered comments and desires of other women circulate. One conversation subtends another and a community of women influencing one another's thoughts and desires instantly comes to life, but only partially. For, as the narrator states in the following paragraph: "D'instinct et de mémoire, j'essaie de ne rien reconstituer" (*PT*f 19) ["From instinct and from memory, I try to reconstruct nothing" (*PT*e 15)]. The reconstruction in question is left to the reader whose gaze upon the screen of words activates them, setting them into mental circulation.

Repeated references to a "white scene" of lovemaking between Michèle Vallée and Claire Dérive punctuate the characters' movements and communications in "The Ordinary," a scene evoked as having "a persistent smell of wood" thus evoking a sensual memory of Djuna Barnes's *Nightwood* (23). The scene takes place on May 16, exactly one month before "Bloomsday" from James Joyce's *Ulysses*, in an unidentified year. As Dawn Thompson has argued: "The light source for the inscription of Brossard's hologram is the sexual intimacy" of the "white scene" even though it resists the status of either the novel's point of origin or teleological end since each repeated evocation shifts or "drifts" according to Claire's surname, and refuses definitive location (23).[3]

The final section is a book-within-a-book with a copyright in the future, from the year 2011, entitled <u>Hologram</u> (*PT*f 173-207, *PT*e 155-184) in keeping with Brossard's "idea of the hologram, which applied to writing prompts me to want to explore a word, an idea, a concept in order to grasp all its dimensions. Just as I have to explore my own subjectivity" (Cotnoir 122). As Susan Knutson explains, a hologram is formed by the interaction of two light beams on a screen, one of which reflects the object to be holographed, which, through a light-wave interference pattern, can reproduce "a three-dimensional image of the holographed object. The holographic screen is reexposed to a laser beam to produce the hologram" (2000 122). Through the light source of the "white scene" together with the illumination of her intertexts,[4] Brossard produces a hologram of "the object to be holographed," namely the extended narrative section at the center of *Picture Theory* entitled "Emotion" which describes five women's island vacation. In the form of a prose poem, <u>Hologram</u> concludes in mid-sentence, inviting the reader, "to reexpose" the narrative "screen" to the light of rereading, to spiral back and reread what came before in this "book" and in the entire novel. She thus elicits the enactment of what she called in "The Aerial Letter" "cette expérience excitante du texte qui tourne autour de lui-même" ["this exciting experience of text which turns about itself"] and then translates "au féminin par un glissement de sens allant de l'excès au délire, du cercle à la spirale" (*LA* 48) ["into the feminine by a shift in meaning going from excess to ecstasy, from circle to spiral" (*AL* 71)].

The first of the two middle sections divides into three books. The first book, entitled "Perspective," is an extended poetic evocation of the "white scene" of love-making in which sense and sensuality merge – "je pensais réellement comme une peau" (*PT*f 71) ["i really thought like a skin"] – and Claire Dérive is compared to the irresistible heroine of *Nightwood* (*PT*e 63). The second "book," "Emotion," takes the form of an extended prose description of a vacation spent on Martha's Vineyard talking about writing, family, and "abstractions" like "reality" and "matriarchy," by five women friends, relatives, and lovers characterized as "studious girls" and as "Border crossers, radical city dwellers, lesbians" (*PT*e 69, 88, 76). "Emotion" radiates from the heart of the novel. Gould emphasizes "emotion" as a "most privileged term" for Brossard which reflects her adherence "to modernity's more general critique of western knowledge and to the debilitating split it has fostered between the body and the intellect" (91). Within "Emotion" Brossard reunites body and intellect. Desire "drifts" in an echo of Brossard's conflation of Pascal's heart with a writing woman's body when Michèle unexpectedly experiences a surge of desire linked to language for her lover's sister Florence, who is also a writer:

> Je regardais Florence Dérive comme un auteur et cela m'évoquait du désir pour elle comme une liaison sonore permet de confondre deux mots et d'en jouir (*PT*f 92).

> I was looking at Florence Dérive like an author and that evoked in me desire for her like a sonorous liaison enabling the m'urging of two words and jouissance (*PT*e 80-81).

A sensation conjoined with reflection rather than a preface to action, desire here leads from "Emotion" to "Thought," the title of the third "book" of the middle section, which consists of short diary-like notes on the narrator's "private Life": "Ma Vie privée est une carte sphérique d'influences et de points de rencontre, elle tourne autour de la langue" (*PT*f 107) ["a spherical map of influences and meeting points, it turns around language" (*PT*e 93)]. With the capitalization of "Life" in "private Life" Brossard emblematizes her theme of women as adult "studious girls" whose inner lives are populated as much by characters from modernist masterpieces like *Finnegan's Wake* (such as Anna Livia Plurabelle) as by personal sentimental preoccupations (*PT*e 91). Such women would "détourn[er] le cours de la fiction, entraînant avec nous les mots tour à tour, spirale ignée, **picture theory**" (*PT*f 99) ["divert the course of fiction, dragging with us words [that] turn and turn about, igneous spiral, **picture theory**" (*PT*e 88)]. In this "book" on "thought" Brossard explains how the writing hologram works: "D'un détail, l'ensemble du continent" (*PT*f 110) ["From one detail, the entire continent" (*PT*e 96)]. From the detail, the overall picture: while women dance inside, "Dehors il neige sur toute l'étendue de la langue" (*PT*f 117) ["Outside it is snowing on the entire expanse of language" (*PT*e 103)]. Turning women are doubled by spinning flakes and words positioned to emulate a hologram.

The second middle section also divides up into three parts: "SCREEN SKIN," "SCREEN SKIN TOO," and "SCREEN SKIN UTOPIA" (in English in the French text). The expression of Michèle's and Claire's ecstatic, utopian meeting comes through skin, through ink and writing, (which was long done on parchment or stretched animal skin), and also through voice, through the ways in which one word ("too") sounds like another ("two"). Brossard's focus on "skin"

linked to "screen," a membrane which can be imprinted or projected upon, with ink or light, and, on a body,
from either side – inside (emotion) or outside (touch)
– highlights her visual and textual play with the idea of
the horizon. In one of the repetitions of the "white
scene" from "The Ordinary," "horizon" is replaced
with its poetic corollary "her/i/zon": a meeting
between equals, between two "I's," each with "her eyes
on" the other, that extends into "l'horizon, jamais je ne
saurai narrer" (*PT*f 26, 24) ["the horizon I will never be
able to narrate" (*PT*e 22, 20)]. "Screen skins" are like
materialized horizons – places where ocean and sky
meet when seen from an island, whether it be Curaçao,
Martha's Vineyard, or Lesbos, and where that natural
light source, the sun, rises and sets.

The homonymy of "SCREEN SKIN TOO," of
"two" in "too" in this second part of the second middle
section, implicitly proposes Simone de Beauvoir's "second sex" as Brossard's answer to the "mémoire patriarcale qui fit croire que la Sphinx pouvait être vaincue par
un homme" (*PT*f 148) ["patriarchal memory that made
people believe the Sphinx could be conquered by a
man" (*PT*e 132)]. This homonymy echoes others in the
text, most notably of the word-name *dérive*- Dérive. It
anticipates the visual homonymy of the two facing blank
pages, in the French language edition, at the beginning
of the last book, <u>Hologramme</u>, which visually "repeat"
the "white scene" (*PT*f 174-5). The ways in which
words sound like other words enact within *Picture*

Theory the polyphonic quality of Brossard's intertextual references, "too," both explicit and implicit, from *Ulysses* and *Finnegan's Wake* to Joyce's story "The Dead" through the presence of swirling snowflakes, Barnes's *Nightwood*, Wittgenstein, Gertrude Stein, Georges Perec, André Breton, and Monique Wittig.[5] Barnes's work may be seen in the impetus of women on the move and felt through the "smell" of wood throughout *Picture Theory* which at times blends with the Steinian odor of roses in the form of "rosewood" (*PT*e 28, 53, 68, 124, see Moyes 1995).[6] These intertexts imbue Brossard's work with a surplus of sensuality – seeing, hearing, touching, smelling. Behind Brossard's Anna, met by chance in Curaçao, for instance, Joyce's Anna Livia Plurabelle lingers, in the references to *Finnegan's Wake* and by name, later on, making sense of the narrator's comment that Anna "sentait la fiction" (*PT*f 105, 29) ["smelled of fiction" (*PT*e 91, 25)].

Sensuality joins abstraction explicitly in the "utopian" third "SCREEN SKIN" section with the double horizon stretching between two thinking women's bodies: "Utopian, against my abstract body I have the sensation of Claire Dérive's body and I articulate some emotions in the room" (*PT*e 137). This utopian horizon, where embodiment and abstraction, ecstasy and text, meet, this Brossardian in-between, grounds epistemology in an ethical relation between equals, between an "I" and a "you," that speaks out through her fiction. The pronouns "I," "you," and "her" punctuate her work, as words binding the writer to her reader and her lover, whose lips, in "The Ordinary," seem to "brush" a poem composed by the narrator, even when she is a continent away (*PT*e 34-35, see Knutson 2002). The utopia of "I" and "you," of "I" and "her," conjured by the holographic convergence of thought with perspective and emotion, renders real the virtual presence of others in the writer's imagination, transforming the singular subject into a social subject continually in relation with others.

For the narrator in *Picture Theory*, as Louise Forsyth affirms, "sees herself as an autonomous although integral part of a coherent and luminous whole, defined completely by the intense energy she generates and shares with other women" in a matrix of interrelationship which has its corollary in space (342). In effect, the space in *Picture Theory* cannot be contained within a linear trajectory but can only be visualized according to the overall pattern of a map, on which it might be possible to see simultaneously Florence Dérive in New York and Montréal, her brother John in New York, his wife in Maine, the narrator in Curaçao (in memory) and in Paris (in body) visiting a holography exhibit, back in Montreal with Claire, and so on – a map that presents a visual rather than a textual image of this "luminous whole" (Forsyth 342).

At the same time that *Picture Theory* invokes a utopian dream of wholeness, of a network of the intersecting trajectories of sensual, thinking women, it resists, self-consciously, the illusion of totalisation. The parts never quite fit into a perfect assembly or, to use Barbara Godard's apt term, "combinatory" of words and images "in which each unit is constantly redeveloped in new combinations" and which, spatially, translates into an "operation of folding, an unfolding to infinity" accompanied by "an infolding of infinity." ("Preface" 8-9). The hologram, after all, is an optical illusion. Brossard evokes it with self-awareness in order to make visible the "horizons" between reality and fiction. Making visible is an important component of her "picture theory" which involves making lesbians visible in a way they mostly have not been in patriarchal histories, allowing them to catch the light like snow flakes at night as they turn, at once individual and collective.[7]

Thompson suggests that Brossard's sense of "the fragmentation of reality" in contemporary "ordinary" life prompts a vision of the world as "a museum of fragments taken out of context precisely by the way we look at it" (39). The ideology of the museum in the nineteenth century, according to Eugenio Donato, was founded on the fiction that "the set of objects the Museum displays [...] somehow constitute a coherent representational universe" as the result "of an uncritical belief in the notion that ordering and classifying, that is to say, the spatial juxtaposition of fragments, can produce a representational understanding of the world" (223). Whereas such juxtaposed fragments could produce a convincing dream of wholeness in the nineteenth-century museum, by the late twentieth-century in *Picture Theory*, illuminated with Brossard's thematisation of illusion, the idea of a "museum of fragments" expresses blanks and silences as much as totality. Going back to Wittgenstein, Brossard presents all the elements necessary for the reader to reconstruct a "picture" of Michèle Vallée's relation to her lover, her friends, and her work while at the same time making us aware of her silences.

The book's many sections repeat and refer to one another, refract each other, intertwining the narrative pieces and characters into a prism that "pictures" as much as tells the converging emotions, desires, memories, and thoughts in a writing woman's life. At one point Brossard even lowers the "screen" of her narrator's "I," referring to Michèle Vallée in the third person and stating: "je savais que derrière elle l'écran serait baissé et qu'elle serait projetée dans mon univers" (*PT*f 165) ["I knew that behind her the screen would be lowered and she would be projected into my universe" (*PT*e 147)]. Behind "woman" as abstraction stands Michèle Vallée, behind whom Brossard thinks and writes, allowing herself, "Nicole Brossard," the authorship of the final book-within-a-book, <u>Hologram</u>.

Brossard situates her *écriture au féminin* "au bout de la nuit patriarcale" ["at the end of patriarchal night"] where body and text fuse in the light of the reader's gaze: "le corps s'anticipe à l'horizon que j'ai devant moi sur un écran de peau, la mienne, dont la résonnance perdure dans ce qui tisse le tissu <u>la lumière</u>" (*PTf* 167) ["the body anticipates on the horizon I have in front of me on the screen of skin, mine, whose resonance endures in what weaves the text / ure t/issue <u>the light</u>" (*PTe* 150)]. Within history while slipping out of it in space-time-mobility, *Picture Theory* is exemplary of feminist fiction from the 1970s and 1980s. Rejecting the masculinist reification of originality with its quotations, the coherence of the singular narrator with its polyphony of voices, and the linear narrative structure of the nineteenth-century novel, Brossard both knowingly follows in the footsteps of her vanguard forebears, from Wittgenstein to Joyce and Barnes, and imagines a new, interactive holographic model for writing and reading, which, with her dance of "I," "you," and "her" invites readers to erect their own holographic maps of the public and private lives of adult, desiring, writing, and mobile "studious girls."

Notes

1. In an interview Brossard confirms: "*Picture Theory* is a novel that I wrote with the feeling of having a three-dimensional consciousness" (Cotnoir 123).

2. See David Edmonds and John Eidinow's *Wittgenstein's Poker* for their presentation of Wittgenstein's questioning of Descartes's *cogito*, which "overturned several hundred years of philosophy" (230), and for more on "language as a tool" (228).

3. In *Narrative in the Feminine* Susan Knutson also argues that "Brossard's text deconstructs the inherent teleology and inherited gender bias of the quest" (115).

4. In this spirit Barbara Godard refers to *Nightwood* as *Lightwood* ("Preface" 8).

5. For more on these intertexts see Lorraine Weir's "From Picture to Hologram" and Liane Moyes's "Caught in Each Other's Dreams." I argue for a surrealist intertext from André Breton's *Nadja* in *Automatic Woman*.

6. For more on mapping in Brossard see Thompson and Huffer.

7. See Godard's "Producing Visibility for Lesbians" for more on Brossard's project of making lesbians visible as "desiring subjects."

Works Cited

Conley, Katharine. *Automatic Woman: The Representation of Woman in Surrealism*. Lincoln, NE: University of Nebraska Press, 1996.

Cotnoir, Louise, Lise Guevremont, Claude Beausoleil and Hugues Corriveau, "Interview with Nicole Brossard on *Picture Theory*." *Canadian Fiction Magazine* 47 (1983): 122-35.

Donato, Eugenio. "The Museum's Furnace: Notes toward a contextual reading of *Bouvard and Pécuchet*." *Textual Strategies*. Ed. Josué Harari. Ithaca: Cornell UP, 1979. 213-38.

Edmonds, David and John Eidinow. *Wittgenstein's Poker*. New York: Ecco Press, 2002.

Forsyth, Louise. "Destructuring Formal Space / Accelerating Motion in the Work of Nicole Brossard." *A Mazing Space*. Eds. Shirley Neuman and Smaro Kamboureli. Edmonton, AB: Longspoon/NeWest, 1986. 334-44.

Godard, Barbara. "Preface." *Picture Theory*. By Nicole Brossard. Montreal: Guernica, 1991. 7- 11.

——. "Producing Visibility for Lesbians: Nicole Brossard's Quantum Physics." *English Studies in Canada* 21.2 (1995): 125-37.

Gould, Karen. *Writing in the Feminine: Feminism and Experimental Writing in Quebec*. Carbondale and Edwardsville: Southern Illinois University Press, 1990.

Huffer, Lynne. *Maternal Pasts, Feminist Futures*. Stanford: Stanford University Press, 1998.

Knutson, Susan. *Narrative in the Feminine*. Waterloo, ON: Wilfrid Laurier University Press, 2000.

——. "Nouns, Pronouns, Verbs 'at eye level': Nicole Brossard's *Jeu de mots* & the Representation of Critical Subjectivity." *Verdure* 56 (February 2002): 112-22.

Moyes, Lianne. "Caught in Each Other's Dreams: Nicole Brossard's Portrait of Djuna Barnes." *Verdure* 56 (February 2002): 91-99.

——. "Composing in the Scent of Wood and Roses." *English Studies in Canada* 21.2 (1995): 206-25.

Perloff, Marjorie. *Wittgenstein's Ladder*. Chicago: University of Chicago Press, 1996.

Thompson, Dawn. *Writing a Politics of Perception: Memory, Holography, and Women Writers in Canada*. Toronto: University of Toronto Press, 2000.

Weir, Lorraine. "From Picture to Hologram: Nicole Brossard's Grammar of Utopia." *A Mazing Space*. Eds. Shirley Neuman and Smaro Kamboureli. Edmonton, AB: Longspoon/NeWest, 1986. 345-52.

Wittgenstein, Ludwig. *Tractatus Logico-Philosophicus*. London: Routledge & Kegan Paul, 1922.

Our Last Chance for Silence

Catherine Campbell

In Michael Ondaatje's *The English Patient* there is a scene describing the primitive pictures of swimmers on a cave wall in the middle of the desert. The people who created them are gone, their way of life is gone – nobody swims there anymore – and yet their mark on the wall, the proof of their existence, remains. When Nicole Brossard says, "je ne fais que porter mon nom dans la cité" (*SA* 16) ["I am simply taking my name into the City" (*SS* 16)], it is with full awareness that women's collective mark has been largely absent from the walls of the city. Much of her work has been an effort to create a space in which women can make that mark. Brossard's approach to the problem is unique in terms of her views of both language and silence. Her concern with both has less to do with the patriarchal sins of the past than how the two can be put to use today. This is not to suggest that those sins have been forgotten. The danger of being silenced looms large in her writing. Despite the potential problems involved, there is an overwhelming sense of silence in her work as the place of primal understanding. Her views have progressed from *Mauve Desert*, in which silence was seen as the place of pure experience but far too dangerous for women, to *Baroque at Dawn* in which the very real danger of losing that silence becomes a concern.

An examination of the inherent tension between language and silence requires a look at two of the underlying assumptions involved. For Brossard women have a closer connection to their physical experience of the world. Men, by nature, are more attracted to the words and the power they represent. Brossard illustrates:

> Ma mère me regarde. Je touche (à) ma mère. C'est évident son corps, je la connais comme une sensation. Lui, pour le connaître, il faut mes yeux. Il faut que je lui parle. Il ne se laisse pas toucher. Il attendra que je puisse parler pour s'intéresser à moi [...] Je ne puis à la fois garder le contact physique avec ma mère et l'écouter lui en même temps (*A* 31).

> My mother looks at me. I am touching my mother. Her body is obvious, I know her like a sensation. But to know him, I need my eyes, I must speak to him. He won't let himself be touched. He'll wait until I can speak before showing interest in me [...] I can't both keep the physical contact with my mother and listen to him at the same time (*TM* 33).

The child's physical knowledge of her mother is at odds with her need to assume a place inside language in order to know her father. The assumption regarding the necessity of sacrificing one type of experience for the other has great implications to the first novel in *Mauve Desert*: <u>Mauve Desert</u>. The second underlying assumption is that reality, as we know it, is created by language. The significance with which Brossard treats this idea increases the importance of women taking a place inside language: "Je sais qu'écrire c'est se faire exister, c'est *comme* décider de ce qui existe et de ce qui n'existe pas, c'est *comme* décider de la réalité" (*LA* 131-2) ["I know that to write is to bring oneself into being; it is *like* determining what exists and what does not, it is *like* determining reality" (*AL* 139)]. Despite the tentative use of the word *like*, the creation and limitations of reality are important to both *Mauve Desert* and *Baroque at Dawn*.

In *Mauve Desert* the struggle out of silence involves two distinct movements: from experience to expression and then from expression to repetition. Both movements are seen as forms of translation. The first, which will be examined here, is Melanie's attempt to express her experience in words, and the second is Maude's attempt to express Melanie's story in another language. Translator Susanne de Lotbinière-Harwood says,

> Toutes les femmes sont bilingues. Nous 'possédons' forcément la langue dominante, de fabrication masculine [...]. Et nous communiquons entre nous dans une langue qui passe par le corps pour se dire et pour s'écrire [...] Traduire nous est donc une activité familière (203-4).

> All women are bilingual. We 'possess' by necessity the dominant language, of masculine creation [...] And we communicate among ourselves in a language which passes through the body to speak and to write [...] Translation for us is, therefore, a familiar activity (my translation).

No matter how vivid the physical experience is, women have no authentic language with which to turn the experience into words. Using patriarchal language is the equivalent of using a second language, leading Brossard to comment that "cette langue étrangère [...] nous la parlons toutes avec *un accent*" (*LA* 90) ["this foreign language [...] is spoken by all of us women with *an accent*" (*AL* 105)].

In *Mauve Desert* the connection between the desert, silence and darkness is stated early by Melanie when she describes the desert as "si chaud, si noir, si blême, silence immense" (*DM* 25) ["so hot, so dark, so pale, immense silence" (*MD* 23)]. Darkness, silence and their physical counterpart, the desert, all represent pre-linguistic space. Melanie, despite her frequent returns to the desert, is in the process of coming out of the desert, the darkness and the silence in order to assume a place inside language. It is notable that she begins to write in the desert and that "la conscience des mots" (26) ["the awareness of words" (24)] occurs during the night.

The first version of Melanie's story deals with the problem of expressing individual experience. She is in the process of discovering life and words and the incongruity of the two. She "[a] quinze ans et le coeur à l'esprit qui s'émerveille" (25) ["[is] fifteen with a heart whose spirit has a sense of wonder" (23)] and she

feels her own existence rather than speaking it or rea-
soning it. The speed of the Meteor, the night, the
desert creatures, and even fear all come to her at the
level of the signified; there is no need for the signifier.
Meaning in the desert has a sort of purity in which she
can "exister sans comparaison" (25) ["exist without
comparison" (23)]. This allusion to the post-structuralist notion of the binary nature of language is clarified by Marxist Terry Eagleton:

> Thus, for male-dominated society, man is the founding
> principle and woman the excluded opposite of this [...]
> But equally man is what he is only by virtue of ceaselessly
> shutting out his other or opposite, defining himself in
> antitheses to it [...] Woman is [...] an other intimately
> related to him as the image of what he is not (132).

Unlike the world of language where she exists only as
a comparison, in the desert she exists in her own right
– without comparison. There she has direct contact not
only with things but with her emotions as well:

> Ici dans le désert, la peur est précise. Jamais obstacle. La
> peur est réelle, n'a rien d'une angoisse [...] Elle est local-
> isée, familière et n'inspire aucun fantasme. Ici, il n'y a que
> du vent, des épines, des serpents, des lycoses, des bêtes, des
> squelettes: la nature même du sol [...] La peur précise est
> belle (*DM* 24).

> Here in the desert, fear is precise. Never an obstacle. Fear
> is real, is nothing like anguish [...] It is localized, familiar
> and inspires no fantasies. Here there are only wind, thorns,

> snakes, wolf-spiders, beasts, skeletons: the soil's very nature [...] Precise fear is beautiful (*MD* 22).

In the desert there is a distinct, precise reason for fear; it is necessary for survival. There is no obstacle between the cause of the emotion and the experience of it and, therefore, no reason to embellish the feeling. Like Melanie herself, emotions exist without comparison. That precision of cause and effect is what she finds beautiful. This type of fear is quite different from the type she feels at home, where "la peur est diffuse" (*DM* 24) ["fear is diffuse" (*MD* 22)]. At the motel, the fear she encounters is not of a primary nature; she has no direct access to the source. She must deal with the emotion as it is translated by others, in this case her mother, who calls it "Une peur blême [...] une peur lente" (*DM* 24) ["A livid fear [...] a slow fear" (*MD* 22)]. Such a fear is vague; it has no specific purpose and, therefore, requires explanation. Speaking about it removes the feeling that much further from its cause and any hope of precision.

This precision represents a directness of meaning that Melanie must return to the silence of the desert over and over again to find. The vast emptiness of the desert is contrasted to the clutter of the motel – the natural is opposed to the man-made. The open space of the desert offers a clarity that she cannot obtain at home. There, in the desert, she can believe in certitudes:

J'étais toujours certaine de tout. Des visages, de l'heure, du ciel, des distances, de l'horizon. J'étais certaine de tout sauf les mots. La peur des mots. Peur lente. Peine à prononcer. Peine à entendre. Peine dans toutes mes veines (*DM* 26).

I was always certain of everything. Of faces, of the time, of the sky, of distances, of the horizon. I was certain of everything except words. The fear of words. Slow fear. Strains to say. Strains to hear. Pain in all my veins (*MD* 23).

It is notable that her fear of words is slow like her mother's fear, suggesting that the words do not have the precision or certitude of her experiences in the desert. The ambiguity of words brings about the same sort of confusion she feels at the motel. "Certitude" clashes with "reality" (13).

In short, the man-made creation, reality, is in opposition to the certainty and pure experience of the desert: "La beauté est avant la réalité [...] je regardais la réalité empiéter sur les êtres comme une distorsion tragique de la beauté" (*DM* 36) ["Beauty is before reality [...] I was watching reality encroach on beings like a tragic distortion of beauty" (*MD* 32)]. Reality is a thing imposed on humanity and it becomes a "petit piège" (*DM* 14) ["little trap" (*MD* 13)]. A person who does not exist within reality created by words does not exist at all. After she begins to write, Melanie thinks, "Je connais la réalité. Je connais l'humanité si soudainement comme une ombre dans mes yeux [...] Depuis que j'avais écrit dans le carnet d'entretien, je voyais vraiment la réalité de près" (*DM* 27) ["I know reality. I know humanity so suddenly like a shadow in my eyes [...] Ever since I had written in the maintenance notebook I could truly see reality close up" (*MD* 24 -25)]. With her new knowledge comes the realization that "les mots peuvent réduire la réalité jusqu'en sa plus petite unité: l'évidence" (*DM* 32) ["words can reduce reality to its smallest unit: *matter* of fact" (*MD* 30)]. Words become the equivalent of a child's building blocks. Reality can be built, taken down, and rebuilt; "La réalité avait un sens, mais lequel?" (*DM* 28) ["Reality had a meaning, but which one?" (*MD* 25)].

The possibility of rebuilding reality is *Mauve Desert*'s most positive message:

> Oui, j'étais fascinée par la réalité et plus précisément par sa dimension impossible. La réalité n'est toujours que le possible accompli et c'est en quoi elle fascine comme un désastre ou offense le désir qui voudrait que tout existe en sa dimension. Je n'étais qu'une forme désirante dans le contour de l'aura qui entourait l'humanité. La réalité est un devenir espacé dans la mémoire. Il faut l'y surprendre comme une forme essentielle (*DM* 37).

> Yes, I was fascinated by reality and more precisely by its impossible dimension. Reality is only ever the possible accomplished and as such it fascinates like a disaster or offends desire which would like for everything to exist in its own dimension. I was nothing but a desiring shape in the contour of the aura surrounding humanity. Reality is a becoming spaced throughout memory. There it must be taken by surprise like an essential shape (*MD* 33).

The impossible dimension of reality coincides with Wittgenstein's notion of what can and cannot be said. That which cannot be said must be left in silence. Since reality has been created by patriarchal language, all of female experience has been left in silence – the impossible dimension. Reality has been the realization of the possible – that which can be expressed by language. This explains why reality is perceived as chaotic by all those who have been excluded from the process. Melanie, however, clearly believes that reality can be reshaped, pushed in another direction: "J'avais quinze ans et de toutes mes forces, j'appuyais sur mes pensées pour qu'elles penchent la réalité du côté de la lumière" (*DM* 14) ["I was fifteen and with every ounce of my strength I was leaning into my thoughts to make them slant reality toward the light" (*MD* 13)].

The fact that there is a choice to be made is illustrated by the change in tense between the first mention of beauty and reality and the second: "La beauté était avant la réalité et la réalité était dans l'écriture, un jour" (*DM* 40) ["Beauty was before reality and reality was in writing, open work" (*MD* 36)]. Melanie is fully aware of the consequences of her choice: "J'ai perdu le désert. J'ai perdu le désert dans la nuit de l'écriture. Il y a toujours une première fois, une première nuit qui brouille les passions, qui confond notre sens de l'orientation" (*DM* 32) ["I lost the desert. I lost the desert in the night of writing. There is always a first time, a first night that blurs passions, that confuses our sense of direction" (*MD* 29)]. In her effort to communicate her experience, she has lost something of the purity and certainty of her connection with the events, surroundings, and emotions. The night of writing may be the literal night she begins to write, but is more likely figurative of a darkness surrounding the activity. She is satisfying "mon désir de l'aube, mon besoin de l'aube" (*DM* 48-9) ["my desire for dawn, my need of dawn" (*MD* 44)] by writing her way out of darkness, towards the light.

In terms of silence, Brossard's stand is quite clear. The positive aspects of silence, represented by Melanie's experiences in the desert, can be very tempting. Especially in the face of the confusion of a *reality* created by words, there is "une volonté de silence" (*DM* 92) ["a will to silence" (*MD* 86)]. But women cannot afford the luxury of retreating from the confusion. "J'étais maintenant entrée dans la peur de l'indicible, dans la fureur des mots sans le vouloir j'abdiquais devant le silence" (*DM* 30) ["I had now entered the fear of the unspeakable, in the frenzy of words involuntarily I was abdicating to silence" (*MD* 28)]. Melanie must overcome the temptation. Words have the power to create *reality* and *reality* is what we all have to live with. Silence is not a viable option.

Although the desert has been exchanged for the sea, the stance taken towards language, reality and silence in *Baroque at Dawn* is very similar to that taken in *Mauve Desert*. Words compromise the possibility of pure experience. The movement out of silence into language has succeeded. The question now is, having gained a position inside language, what is being done with it. *Baroque at Dawn* examines the power and abuses of language as exercised by both genders and the process of creating fiction/reality. Access to the positive aspects of silence that women denied themselves in *Mauve Desert* is now a possibility. Silence begins to take shape as the only viable alternative to the confusion created by language. The concern now is that, in the midst of the noise into which language can deteriorate, we are losing the ability to hear the silence.

Baroque at Dawn goes much farther than *Mauve Desert* in defining the connections among language, fiction and reality. In a rather postmodern move, history becomes one of the metanarratives whose ability to depict reality comes under scrutiny. That which we consider the history of humanity is merely fiction piled upon fiction:

> Chaque altercation engendrait de nouveaux mots [...] Maquillage, tatouage, perçage et débordement de sens se succédaient. La vie trébuchait sur les valeurs nouvelles [...] Les générations se succédaient (*BA* 43).

> Each altercation generated new words [...] Face-painting, tattooing, body-piercing, sensual overkill came one after the next. Life stumbled over values that were new [...] Generations passed one after the next (*BD* 35) .

In the same way that the histories of the world have created a collective reality, a person's own stories make up his or her individual reality. As La Sixtine tells Cybil, "Avouez-le: personne n'existe en dehors de son récit" (*BA* 28) ["Nobody exists outside her own story – admit it" (*BD* 20)]. Whereas the personal histories of many of the characters in *Mauve Desert* were carefully concealed, the pages of *Baroque at Dawn* are littered with such stories. The reader is even given the background of minor characters such as the Demers brothers. From the beginning when La Sixtine asks, "Voulez-vous que je vous interprète ma vie?" (*BA* 28) ["Would you like me to play you my life?" (*BD* 21)] to the end when Occident, on the last night of her life, tells her own story, each character is driven to offer some explanation for how he or she has arrived at this moment.

While telling one's story may seem harmless, the act as presented here is less than benevolent. At its worst it is actually a form of assault which varies in intensity. At the milder end of this scale, the words of one person merely overwhelm another as happens when Irene and a male friend share stories of their grief:

> Avec le temps, ses paroles se transformèrent en de longs monologues qu'il m'était de plus en plus difficile d'interrompre par une question, une remarque, une opinion.

Chaque fois que j'ouvrais la bouche, ses mots avaient tôt fait d'engloutir les miens [...] (*BA* 91-2).

With time, the talk turned into long monologues which I found harder and harder to interrupt with a question, observation or opinion. Every time I opened my mouth, his words would very soon engulf mine (*BD* 83).

This is inconsiderate but not malicious. The character is driven by a need to speak and not a desire to dominate the other person. Not all exchanges are as innocent. At the most severe end of the scale a person can be dragged into the story of another and held captive there. An assault of this nature takes place when Cybil finds herself left at the mercy of fellow dinner guest James Warland: "L'homme t'entraîne au bout du monde. Il tapisse l'espace de descriptions fines. Vous visitez des palais, des ruines, au milieu de la jungle [...] Vous marchez au milieu des guerres et des révolutions" (*BA* 116) ["He takes you to the far corners of the earth, setting each scene with fine descriptions. You visit palaces, ruins deep in the jungle [...]You walk amid wars and revolutions" (*BD* 109)]. The aftermath of the "délire de l'homme" ["man's delirium"] leaves her "dans un mutisme sans égal" (*BA* 118) ["mute as never before" (*BD* 111)].

Despite the importance given to the telling of stories, Cybil points out that there is a sharp difference between knowing a person's story and knowing a person: "Il faut plus qu'une histoire pour comprendre les êtres" (*BA* 28) ["You need more than a story if you're going to understand people" (*BD* 20)]. One can only genuinely know another – pure experience – if language – names and stories – is avoided. This is why Cybil attempts to have anonymous encounters with strange women. The moment language enters, fiction takes over. The narrator claims that "[c]onnaître le passé de quelqu'un, c'est le déposséder de son présent" (*BA* 62) ["[k]nowing someone's story amounts to depriving her of her present" (*BD* 54)]. The real person fades into the background and a character is born. The character of La Sixtine continues to visit Cybil long after the person is gone. Cybil, therefore, does not relent to La Sixtine's request for a story. Later at a concert while "le plaisir [cru] des sons" ["the [raw] pleasure of the sounds"] causes her to enjoy a feeling that is "présent, réel, très physique" ["present, real, and very physical"] she reflects, "C'est parce que je suis heureuse que j'ai refusé à la Sixtine une histoire" (*BA* 45) ["It's because I'm happy that I refused to give La Sixtine a story" (*BD* 37)]. She is reluctant to let words clutter the experience of the moment. Two strangers can meet without the "récit que chacune porte en elle. Il y a là une économie de l'histoire au profit de la présence" ["background baggage carried by each. Less of the past benefits an immediate presence"]. And presence "sert à la conscience [...] permet [...] d'exercer cette merveilleuse faculté en nous qui est de produire du sens à partir de nos sens" (*BA* 26-7) ["makes one more aware [...] lets you [...] use that marvellous capacity we have of producing sense with our senses" (*BD* 19)].

The juxtaposition of the pure experience with the confusion of reality created by language is a repetition of the paradox illustrated by *Mauve Desert*. However, in *Baroque at Dawn* time becomes an important consideration. The fictions that constitute the past have already been mentioned. The future has a similar affinity to fiction: "Le futur nous enracine dans la fiction" ["The future roots us in fiction"], for even the best laid plans can be no more than speculation. Both excite and tempt the imagination: "Au futur [...] le caractère effrayant de notre aptitude au voyage et au vertige des grands espaces et de la promiscuité" ["When the future comes [...] there's always this extraordinary capacity of ours for voyaging, the excitement of open spaces and random mingling"]. However, the temptation of endless possibilities makes the future "une rumeur continue qui intoxique l'énergie du présent, nous tient constamment sur nos gardes" (*BA* 229) ["a constant rumour that poisons present energy and keeps us continually on our guard" (*BD* 225)].

Given the fictional nature of past and future, it makes sense that the only pure experience possible is within the present. As in *Mauve Desert,* pure experience is equated with the physical and so, therefore, is the present: "Le présent est un corps. Le corps est vivant, pur présent" (*BA* 23) ["The present is a body. The body is a live, pure present" (*BD* 15)]. Music also holds the power of creating a physical sensation capable of tying a body to the present. At a concert the music of the tango causes "une indicible sensation de présent. Un fabuleux présent qui contient tous les plis de la douleur, de la solitude et du bonheur roulés au fond de toi" (*BA* 120-1) ["an unutterable feeling of here and now. A fabulous present containing all the folds of pain and solitude and happiness rolled together deep inside you" (*BD* 114)]. Finally a physical experience, the feeling of the wind, allows Cybil to "étrein[dre] bien fort le présent" (*BA* 115) ["hold tight to the present" (*BD* 108)].

One of the things that jeopardizes her hold on the present and the pure experience of the moment is language. The most notable example occurs during a particularly vocal meal on board the ship. What ensues is "La confusion [...] La langue était comme une grande folle assoiffée de rêves" ["Bedlam [...] language behaving like a certified crackpot starved for dreams"]. During this incident, as at other times, language literally takes on a life of its own: "elle avalait, vite, goulûment [...] petites et grandes histoires [...] Inassouvissable [...] La langue tourbillonnait, ouragan fou, trombe d'eau. La langue avalait son propre déluge" ["it gulped down everything, all stories great and small, rapidly and with relish [...] Language was spinning uncontrolled like a hurricane, a waterspout. Language was drinking a flood of its own making"]. The personification of language as a beast spinning out of control also raises a concern over women throwing themselves too completely into its clutches. Although *Mauve Desert* advocates taking a place inside language at any cost, the message of *Baroque at Dawn* is to proceed with caution. Language as an entity can be "sans merci" ["merciless"] and must be handled with great care: "Il fallait beaucoup d'amour pour que la langue nous enivre sans nous plonger dans le chaos [...] Elle ne pardonne pas si on l'écarte ou la désire distraitement" (*BA* 141-2) ["We would have to give language a lot of love to have it exhilarate us without drowning us in the chaotic spate of words [...] Nor will it forgive being ignored or courted absentmindedly" (*BD* 135-6)]. The last refuge from a world entirely under the power of language is silence.

In many ways the entity that language becomes acts as a foil for the entity that silence becomes. Cybil experiences a silence "épouvantablement vivant" (*BA* 18) ["terribly alive" (*BD* 11)], so much so that it beckons her; "Le silence épelle son nom dans la chambre" (*BA* 69) ["The silence in the room spells out her name." (*BD* 61)]. And as with language, it is possible to lose control of the beast: "Sixtine, le silence tourbillonne" (*BA* 74) ["Sixtine, the silence is spinning" (*BD* 66)]. However, the creature *silence* is, in all cases, more benevolent than the creature *language*:

> Lentement, le silence fait son apparition. Plus lentement encore, il fait son personnage. Alors, il capte toutes l'atten-

tion [...] Le silence marche en tenant Cybil par la main; il
l'entraîne dans un espace à ciel ouvert (*BA* 71).

Slowly, the silence makes its appearance. More slowly still,
it makes like a character. Then it monopolizes attention
[...] The silence takes Cybil by the hand and walks, leading
her to a place open to the sky" (*BD* 63).

Despite the similarities suggested by the personification of the two concepts, language and silence are at
opposite ends of the spectrum. Language takes shape
to confuse an existing situation. Silence, on the other
hand, takes shape in order to lead Cybil in the direction
of clarity.

Unlike the earlier novel, there is now a marked distinction between this greater more universal type of
silence and a more individual type. From a Brossardian
point of view individual silence would now be the most
problematic. Although women have free access to various degrees and uses of this type, there remains a danger of being driven back into silence and trapped there,
as James Warland manages to do with Cybil. Perhaps
the most disturbing example of how men can still use
this type of silence against women is to be found in one
of the virtual reality programs of the Demers brothers.
They recreate their dead mother's bedroom where they
can go to watch "maman dort, maman se maquille,
maman change de robe, maman regarde par la fenêtre"
(*BA* 170) ["Maman [...]sleeping or putting on her
makeup or changing her dress or looking out the win-

dow" (*BD* 166)]. The only thing the woman cannot do is leave the room – or speak. When Cybil visits the room, she finds "[s]a bouche est pleine de murmures et de chuchotements comme pour bien s'assurer du passage des mots de l'oeil à la bouche, puis au coeur. Quelque chose ne va pas" (*BA* 186-7) ["Her mouth is full of whispers and murmurings as if she's making sure the words get from her eye to her mouth, then to her heart. Something's wrong" (*BD* 183)].

However, women are no longer merely the victims of this type of silence; they can now retreat voluntarily into their own silence. Women's ability to move from language to silence is demonstrated by a scene in which Irene is dominating the conversation. Just when Cybil has given up hope of stopping her, "voilà qu'elle expose fièrement son silence comme d'autres un argument. Le silence ondule, ruban de nostalgie" (*BA* 127) ["lo and behold she brings out her silence as others do an argument. Like a ribbon of nostalgia, the silence undulates" (*BD* 120-1)]. The comparison of silence to both nostalgia and an argument implies that silence contains meaning similar to language.

Perhaps because they no longer feel themselves in control of the situation, men now feel threatened by the silence of women. As the women gradually withdraw from the dinnertime conversations, the men become more and more uncomfortable:

> Irène ne participait plus à la conversation [...] Occident interrompait de moins en moins les hommes. Pour ma

part, je m'enfermais dans un silence qui, au fur et à mesure
que je m'y enfonçais, ruinait en moi tout espoir de socia-
bilité. Thomas Lemieux n'aimait pas notre silence. Il y
voyait complot, reproche, rejet, je ne sais quoi (*BA* 179).

Irene had ceased to take part in the conversation [...]
Occident was interrupting the men less and less often. For
my own part, I was locked in a silence which, the further I
sank into it, the more surely ruined all hope of sociability
in me. Thomas Lemieux did not like our silence. He saw
in it a plot, reproach, rejection, I don't know which (*BD*
175).

The most self-serving intentional use of silence takes
place when Cybil stops talking in order to avoid having
to tilt her head back when responding to an extremely
tall friend (*BA* 105, *BD* 97). While, as noted earlier,
Cybil argues that it is impossible to know another person through language, she acknowledges the possibility of doing so through silence. She reflects that the
essence of another can be visible, but "il fallait toucher
tout de très près, à la vitesse du vivant, et attendre que
la femme dispose de son propre silence à bout de souf-
fle et de syllabes, au milieu de son présent" (*BA* 20)
["she would have to consider everything very carefully
at the speed of life and wait for the woman to possess
her own silence, out of breath and beyond words in the
midst of her present" (*BD* 12)]. She later affirms that
"oui le silence rapproche" (*BA* 257) ["yes, silence
draws people together" (*BD* 253)].

The most striking aspect in the evolution of silence

from *Mauve Desert* to *Baroque at Dawn* is its position in respect to language. In the earlier novel clinging to silence jeopardized one's ability to take a place inside language. The positive aspects of silence were acknowledged but considered expendable, albeit regretfully. Now clinging to language jeopardizes one's ability to take a place inside silence. *Baroque at Dawn* takes a closer look at the positive aspects and questions the wisdom of sacrificing them. The narrator warns, "La mer est notre dernier silence" ["The sea is our last chance for silence"]. Whereas in *Mauve Desert,* the desert was the physical equivalent of silence, in *Baroque at Dawn* it is the sea. There are obvious similarities between the two: both are vast, timeless and beyond compare – "Au bord de la mer, je suis d'une superbe incommensurable" (*BA* 93) ["Beside the sea I'm superbly immeasurable" (*BD* 85)]. They also both offer the possibility of pure experience. Cybil declares they have gone to sea "pour le corps, pour que l'esprit s'abandonne au vent, au silence et à la nuit" (*BA* 135) ["so our bodies and minds can give way to the wind and the silence and the night" (*BD* 130)].

Brossard allows for the possibility of finding a balance between language and silence. Although in danger, the sea and silence are still within our reach:

> Un seul corps pour satisfaire l'envie de lumière et de mer. Un seul corps pour trouver les mots nécessaires, pour nous obliger à répéter [...] Corps de mémoire pour inventer et progresser vers le silence. (*BA* 219).

One single body to satisfy our craving for light and sea.
One single body for finding the necessary words and oblig-
ing us to repeat them [...] A body of memory for inventing
and progressing toward silence (*BD* 215).

Balance is, nonetheless, a possibility, not a probability.
And the cost of making the mark on the wall must be
considered.

Les pensées changent-elles de nature parce que le corps
attrape à d'autres niveaux le sens de la vie? Le corps peut-
il simultanément faire attention aux choses universelles, à
la couleur de l'aube et laisser faire la fiction? Qu'allons-
nous chercher dans le silence d'autrui? (*BA* 260)

Does the nature of our thoughts change because the body
grasps the meaning of life on other planes? Can the body
pay attention to the colour of the dawn and to things universal at the same time, and let fiction roll as well? [...]
What are we to look for in the silence of others [...]? (*BD*
256)

Or as she asks elsewhere, "How many trips to the sea
to imagine what silence will be one day?" (Brossard
and Marlatt 5).

Works Cited

Brossard, Nicole and Daphne Marlatt. "Only a Body to Measure Reality By: Writing
the in-Between." *Journal of Commonwealth Literature* 31 (1996): 5-17.

Eagleton, Terry. *Literary Theory: An Introduction.* Oxford: Basil Blackwell Ltd., 1983.

Lotbinière-Harwood, Susanne de. "Re-belle et infidèle: la traduction comme pratique
de réécriture au féminin." *Les discours féminins dans la littérature postmoderne au
Québec.* Eds. Raija Koski, Kathleen Kells, & Louise Forsyth. New York: The
Edwin Mellen Press, 1993. 202- 217.

Ondaatje, Michael. *The English Patient.* New York: Knopf, 1992.

Feminist Legends of Natureculture

Brossard, Haraway, Science

SUSAN KNUTSON

In over thirty-five years of writing, Nicole Brossard has produced a profound body of work that has transformed reading communities internationally, wherever her texts have been received and studied. As she has animated and transgressed the boundaries of poetry, fiction and theory, she has never ceased to take risks to discover "La langue [en tant que] spectacle de ce que nous ne pouvons pas penser comme *telles*" (*PT*f 183) ["Language [as] a spectacle of what we cannot think as *such (women)*" (*PT*e161)]. Her texts point to the virtual virtuosity of the mind engaging with multi-dimensional language, generating the electromagnetic pageantry of *thinking*, throwing off death, learning, being fully human. Strikingly, in her sustained attention to scientific knowledge, including brain science, wave theory, mathematics, optics and computer science, Brossard stands in a relationship of *consilience* to the most powerful knowledge practices of our time.[1] Her writing explores reality and discovers new and accurate tropes for human-being-in-the-world.

As early as the 1982 text "Synchronie" (*LA* 79-85) ["Synchrony" (*AL* 97-101)], she points to the importance of scientific knowledge for poetry: "Ainsi voit-on surgir d'inédites métaphores ayant partie liée avec le cerveau: l'hologramme, l'ordinateur" (82) ["we are witnessing the appearance of entirely new metaphors, some associated with the brain: the hologram, the computer" (99)]. In an interview recorded in Montréal in the summer of 1988, she elaborates the idea that revolutionary advances in science and technology have become sites of discovery for new tropic interpretive structures based on aspects of nature that are not visible to the naked eye, "*des ondes, des vibrations*":

> We live in general in our society with metaphors which belong to the industrial and agricultural periods. We don't live with the metaphors of our new technology, and I think that the new technology provides us with information which somehow we will fantasize. When we do, then we'll come up with new metaphors which will tell more about space and time, will tell about them in a different way. There are things we can do because of gravity, and now we are discovering things we can do without gravity, and we will be able to do them. It's very challenging. Just the fact that we know so little about the brain – we can imagine a certain potential. It doesn't mean that we would be happier; it only means that we can dream (Personal interview, June 8, 1988).

Her comments leave no doubt of her interest not only in the technological achievements of science but in the scientific explorations of the human brain, the consilient relatedness of the brain's activities in the production of consciousness and the technological production of virtual realities and holographic images. As she notes, the hologram in particular can represent consciousness and technoscientific achievement in the world. For this reason, the semiotically potent hologram best serves as a point of departure for an analysis of Brossard's metaphoric sourcing of science, and her pivotal 1982 novel *Picture Theory* most naturally serves as the focus of investigation.

The hologram, and one hologram in particular, is the ultimate "picture" referred to by the title *Picture Theory*. The governing image of the novel and the inspiration and model for its radical non-linear narrative structure, the hologram has its special place among the repertoire of figures such as the dawn, the white centre, travel and translation, that Brossard has developed and imbued with layers of meaning over a period of many years.[2] As a trope related to light, to thought, and to language, the hologram of *Picture Theory* gives deeper sense to *Aube à la saison* and *Le centre blanc*, and satisfies the complex desire which is the final expression of *These Our Mothers*: "Je veux *en effet* voir s'organiser la forme des femmes dans la trajectoire de l'espèce" (99) ["I want to see *in fact* the form of women organizing in the trajectory of the species" (101)]. Looking in the direction of *Mauve Desert*, the hologram illuminates the figure of translation – an encounter between two fields of language, and a transformation which is *making sense* – that dominates Brossard's writing in the late 1980s.

Picture Theory's narrative architecture is based on the repetition of an event unit modeled on the light wave interference patterns, which *as technology*, produce three-dimensional holograms, and *as nature*, produce "holographic" pictures or meanings in the brain (see Pribram). The textual fiction, or fiction theory, brings the two sides of the coin together with feminist intention, sexual ecstasy, emotion and thought. The brain, reaching after a more complete sense of what women might yet be, achieves, in the process of reading the text, a certain potential. Each element of the story demands rereading.

As technology, the three-dimensional holographic image is a twentieth-century triumph in the history of optics, a history which begins with the diffraction of light rays as they pass through a tiny space and are reconstituted as an upside-down image of that to which those rays have been exposed. This remarkable natural phenomenon, which makes possible the *camera obscura*, was known to the ancient Greeks and Chinese, and used by Arab astronomers in the tenth century and by European artists during the Renaissance. Images created with the *camera obscura* are roughly captured, upside-down, cloudy and dark. However, the technology progressed, the lens was discovered, and by the nineteenth century, the era of the first feminist wave, cameras such as the Giroux daguerreotype camera (1839), made by Alphonse Giroux of Paris, were widely sold to the public. In 1948,

Hungarian scientist Denis Gabor made the first holo-gram, for which he was awarded the Nobel Prize in 1971. Holograms are produced by splitting a beam of light into a reference beam and another that reflects the object to be holographed. The two light beams interact on a filter or screen, creating a light wave interference pattern that can reproduce, under appropriate condi-tions, a three-dimensional image of the holographed object. In the 1960s, holographs began to be made with laser light characterized by coherent wave patterns; the holographic screen is reexposed to a laser beam to pro-duce a hologram. Today there are many kinds of holo-grams integrated into the technological fabric of our culture. At the optics installation at the Science Museum in London, England, a similar summary his-tory of optics culminates with a hologram of Dr. Denis Gabor.

Picture Theory tells the story of optics *in the femi-nine*, so that the *camera obscura* speaks to us allegori-cally of the difficulty and darkness surrounding women's self-representations, and the middle distance is connoted by the hippie photographers at Pamela Judith's wedding, in the era that brought us the second wave of the women's movement, and anti-war and civil rights activism. Major narrative events such as the island vacation and the love-making of Michèle and Claire parallel the technology of hologram production: a beam of light (the plural feminist subject) that has been exposed to what will be reproduced (a more meaningful idea of *woman*), is separated into two parts, which subsequently reunite, producing energy. The summation is the hologram of *the integral woman*.

Evidently, light wave interference patterns are not created exclusively or even primarily by human technology. They occur in nature. Interference patterns of electromagnetic waves may constitute the virtual reality of consciousness in the brain. Brossard's readers will recognize many key Brossardian terms – such as parallel, relay, synchrony, cortex, memory – in E.O. Wilson's description of the processes of consciousness:

> Consciousness consists of the parallel processing of vast numbers of [...] coding networks. Many are linked by the synchronized firing of the nerve cells at forty cycles per second, allowing the simultaneous internal mapping of multiple sensory impressions. Some of the impressions are real, fed by ongoing stimulation from outside the nervous system, while others are recalled from the memory banks of the cortex. All together they create scenarios that flow realistically back and forth through time. The scenarios are a virtual reality. They can either closely match pieces of the external world or *depart indefinitely from it*. They re-create the past and cast up alternative futures that serve as choices for future thought and bodily action (120, my emphasis).

In Brossard's feminist text, it is of course a question of *departing indefinitely from* the patriarchal world, changing (raising) consciousness and creating new *choices for future thought and bodily action*. "Le patriarcat n'aura pas lieu, dois-je l'énoncer?" (*PT*f 22) ["The patriarchy shall not take place, should I state it?" (*PT*e 18)]. The material from memory is "screened" by the lesbian skin which seeks exposure to positive images of women: there is a refusal to reconstruct the past. "D'instinct et de mémoire, j'essaie de ne rien reconstituer" (*PT*f 19) ["From instinct and from memory, I try to reconstruct nothing" (*PT* 15)].

The parallel processes involved in changing consciousness and producing the hologram are meta-narrated by the chapter structure of *Picture Theory*, which moves through the "Ordinary" to "Perspective," "Emotion," "Thought," "Screen Skin," "Screen Skin Too," and "Screen Skin Utopia" to *another book* (21), which is *Hologram* (161-188).

Brossard clarifies the meaning of this narrative movement in "Mémoire: Hologramme du désir," a text composed for the Third International Feminist Book Fair at l'Université de Montréal in 1988. Focussing on the double sense of the word *légende* [legend], as 1) a text that accompanies an image, and 2) a narrative based in fact, but transformed by time, she argues that "[c]e n'est que lorsque nous pouvons dire la légende de nos vies que nous devenons capables d'engendrer des scènes nouvelles, d'inventer de nouveaux personnages, de produire de nouvelles répliques, nous frayant ainsi un chemin dans le présent" ["it is only when women are able to narrate the *legends* of our lives that we become capable of engendering new scenes, inventing new characters, producing new responses, and so creating a pathway for ourselves in the present" (6)]. "L'éclairage narratif" ["narrative lighting" (6)] is a required production value if one is to stage, in the body itself – "le théâtre premier de la représentation ["the first theatre of representation] – "des élans de joie qui enthousiasment la pensée" [...] waves of joy that exhilarate thought"(6)], and which are necessary for the production of the hologram.

The hologram is *la femme intégrale*, *"la" femme*, or Woman, semantically charged as an ideal, utopic expression, not to be confused with actual women. *Intégrale* [*integral*]: complete, entire; the *Petit Robert* offers this forceful definition for the word: *qui n'est l'objet d'aucune diminution, d'aucune restriction* [that which is not the object of any diminution or restriction."As a representation of women without diminution, *la femme intégrale* calls up feminist aspirations towards social justice and human rights for actual women around the world. She is also a lover, and *Picture Theory* suggests that her energy is emotion. "Brain scientists [...] have established that passion is inseverably linked to reason. Emotion is not just a perturbation of reason but a vital part of it" (*Consilience* 116). And in the passionately, radically feminist world of *Picture Theory*, the beloved is a woman.

La femme intégrale is a political trope: a lesbian feminist as paradigmatic human, a lesbian human generic. This does not mean that she must be read as a Female Universal in the sense of a sign which would mask or curtail the rights of other genders or signs. Read her, rather, as whole and sufficient in what she is. Her potentially conflictual relationship with traditional patriarchal symbolic and social structures stems from the predication of those structures on the exchange of women between male subjects. Like Louky Bersianik's *L'Euguélionne*, *la femme intégrale* seeks the positive of her species rather than an *agon* to complete her.

As a generically female **M**an, as a figure who stands at the intersection of Big Science and human bodies and emotions, the hologram of the integral woman is neither nature nor culture but a representation of both at the threshold of the future. She is in this sense comparable to the border figures created by American feminist philosopher of science, Donna Haraway. In particular, the hologram might be good company for Haraway's FemaleMan©.

The FemaleMan©, "Modest witness" and OncoMouse™ are figures from Haraway's 1997 book, *Modest_Witness @Second_Millennium.FemaleMan©_Meets_OncoMouse™: Feminism and Technoscience*, where they "stand in for new ways of imagining and doing technoscience." (*How Like a Leaf* 158) The FemaleMan© is the chief figure of feminism, based, as Haraway explains (*Leaf* 170), on Joanna Russ's 1975 novel *The Female Man*, a book that "is the antithesis of topian or dystopian novel; the book, in form and content, is the disruption of the expectations of those and many other central gendered categories of linguistic production in white European and American writing technologies" (*Modest_Witness* 70). Brossard, Haraway and Russ, while parting company with respect to the value of the utopian tradition in fiction, are alike in creating figures that point to the ontological violence of the masculine generic from the point of view of female human beings.

All three authors address the implicit question: how, when Man is unavailable, can we represent the female as fully human? The expressions chosen point to the inherent contradiction separating, by definition, the generic from the distinguishing mark: "the generic that must be qualified does not count as a self-contained type with its own natural telos; s/he is a generic scandal." (*Modest_Witness* 71) S/he displays the contamination of the natural. Like Haraway's Cyborg, and like the female clones who populate Russ's novel, Brossard's hologram of *la femme intégrale* displays the implosion of nature and culture, which, from one point of view, makes her a kind of monstrosity. But feminists are familiar with the ideological mechanisms of representation which have turned rebellious or women-loving women into monstrosities: blue stockings, new women, mannish women, *tribades*, unnatural women. Surely this is a sinister but not uncommon manifestation of the false concretizations which commonly "misrepresent complexity, misrepresent process and instead fetishize, fix, reify 'complexity' into 'things'" (*Leaf* 21)? Haraway is speaking here of the misrepresentation of nature by the discourse of biology, but the mechanism she is discussing is more widespread than that and her terms are taken, as she explains, from Alfred North Whitehead's discussion of the "fallacy of misplaced concreteness" by means of which people habitually present themselves "with simplified editions of immediate matters of fact" (Whitehead 52; cited in *Leaf* 117). As Whitehead notes, people do this in order to get through their days without really thinking; Brossard, however, as a writer, is particularly committed to provoking thought: "fresh sequences of / the voice and its belonging," as she is also particularly opposed to reiterating calcified language: "the way we talk to / neighbours before we buy / a newspaper or a coffee / hollow hello" ("A Blind Chameleon," 38-39).

Brossard and Haraway both reject the patriarchal paradigm of the "natural woman" while reinscribing women's place in the whole of nature/culture that we are immersed in. Haraway explains: "what I'm interested in most are 'naturecultures' – as one word – implosions of the discursive realms of nature and culture. Within this context I have written about cyborgs, on the one hand, and animals on the other, specifically about primates" (*Leaf* 105). Approaching this matter as a poet, Brossard creates dense cyborgian signs such as *la femme intégrale*. She delineates the complex metaphoric relatedness linking hologram production to the textuality of feminist fiction theory and its reception in the human brain. She names "Memory:

Hologram of Desire," and our bodies as "museums of bone and water." In "The Vast Complication of Beauty" she writes of our deep kinship with the sea:

> aujourd'hui je sais que la structure la plus bleue de la mer se rapproche de nos cellules et de la souffrance intouchable comme la vie fait trois fois le tour de notre enfance sans jamais y toucher vraiment parce qu'on est proche de la réalité et que la matière ne peut pas tomber sans nous avertir, nous laisser là, la peau hésitante entre les philosophies et l'aube, à moitié, à jamais dans le tourment, dans la vaste complication de la beauté (*PV* 109).

> today I know that the deepest blue structure of the sea comes close to our cells and untouchable suffering as life circles around our childhood three times without ever really touching it because we are close to reality and matter cannot fall without warning us, leaving us there, skin hesitating between philosophies and the dawn, halfway, forever in torment, in the vast complication of beauty (trans. LHF).

Haraway, too, has reflected on our deep physical kinship not only with other animals but with the cellular processes of the natural world. She responds with an image of this when, during her interview with Thyrza Nichols Goodeve, she is asked: "what are the moments when you remember [your experience of "cyborgness"] crystallizing for you?":

> Well, one is certainly my sense of the intricacy, interest, and pleasure – as well as the intensity – of how I have imagined how like a leaf I am. For instance, I am fascinated with the

molecular architecture that plants and animals share, as well as with the kinds of instrumentation, interdisciplinarity, and knowledge practises that have gone into the historical possibilities of understanding how I am like a leaf (131-132).

Tracing the "very potent join between fact and fiction" (*Leaf* 50), both authors use scientific information to discover non-reductionist "metaphors that deal with complex wholes and complex processes" (*Leaf* 50).

Nicole Brossard and Donna Haraway have in some respects worked in parallel, and there are many other possible points of comparison between their bodies of work. For example, like Brossard, Haraway is interested in light diffraction theory, which she proposes as a metaphor for critical consciousness, because of its inscription of complexity and process:

> [W]hen light passes through slits, the light rays that pass through are broken up. And if you have a screen at one end to register what happens, what you get is a record of the passage of the light rays onto the screen. This "record" shows the history of their passage through the slits. So what you get is not a reflection; it's the record of a passage" (*Leaf* 103).

And, like Haraway, Brossard is interested in what science and technology can reveal about who we are and where we are living today. Born months apart to North American Catholic families in the 1940s, both writers are today at the forefront of articulating and rethinking what it means to be human and female, in our time. This is not because they have been influenced by one another, nor is it because they are part of the same discursive community, although, in this global world, they are, of course, in some sense. But their kinship as writers and philosophers comes about primarily because they have both responded critically but without denial to the scientific and technological revolution that has changed what we as human beings are. Their ideas illuminate this real conjuncture of human-being-in-the-world.

Notes

1. In *Consilience,* E.O. Wilson cites William Whewell, who, in *The Philosophy of the Inductive Sciences* (1840), was the first to speak of consilience: "literally, a 'jumping together' of knowledge by the linking of facts and fact-based theory across disciplines to create a common groundwork of explanation" (6).
2. I have written about Brossard's repertoire of tropes in "Reading Nicole Brossard," and about the narrative structure of *Picture Theory* in *Narrative in the Feminine: Daphne Marlatt and Nicole Brossard.*

Works Cited

Bersianik, Louky. *L'Euguélionne.* Montréal: La Presse, 1976. Wildeman. 97-101.

Haraway, Donna J. *How Like a Leaf: An Interview with Thyrza Nichols Goodeve.* New York: Routledge, 2000.

——. *Modest_Witness@Second_Millennium.FemaleMan© _Meets_ OncoMouse™: Feminism and Technoscience.* New York: Routledge, 1997.

Knutson, Susan. *Narrative in the Feminine: Daphne Marlatt and Nicole Brossard.* Waterloo: Wilfrid Laurier University Press, 2000.

——. "Reading Nicole Brossard." *Ellipse* 53 (Spring, 1995): 9-19.

Pribram, Karl. *Languages of the Brain: Experimental Paradoxes and Principles in Neuropsychology.* Englewood Cliffs, N.J.: Prentice-Hall, 1971.

Whitehead, Alfred North. *Science and the Modern World.* New York: Mentor Books, 1948.

Wilson, Edward O. *Consilience: The Unity of Knowledge.* London: Abacus, 1998.

Delirious Translations in the Works of
Nicole Brossard

Susan Holbrook

Délire appears in Nicole Brossard's *Amantes* both as a
single word and in the recurrent, punning statement,
"JE N'ARRÊTE PAS DE LIRE" (11). The pun, a
notoriously untranslatable figure, is spelled out in the
English *Lovhers* as "I DON'T STOP READING /
DELIRING" (19). In the French, *délire* (or *de lire*) signifies variously as *reading*, *delirium* and, as translator
Barbara Godard points out, "dé-lire, to unread or unfix
reading" (11). Unable to accommodate this particular
semantic cluster within one English word, Godard
concretizes the bipolar constitution of the pun by plac-
ing "reading" and "deliring" on either side of a virgule.
This slashed construction marks the operation of
translation, not only in its bifurcation of the pun, but
also in its exhibition of what appears to be an angli-
cized French word resulting in an English neologism.
Indeed, *deliring* is nowhere to be found in dictionaries
of contemporary English usage, and thus functions as
an instance of foreignicity, a nod both to the linguistic
specificity of the first version and to the translator's
labour. An etymological dig, however, reveals that the
verb *delire* was once in English circulation, losing
ground only at the end of the seventeenth century.
Delire meant "to go astray, go wrong, err," and was

derived, like the French, from the Latin *delirare*: "to go out of the furrow, to deviate from the straight." When Brossard deploys *délire* in its unbroken form, Godard translates it literally as *delirium*, a word which is also derived from *delirare* and signifies a "frenzied rapture" (OED 679).

Brossard invokes *délire* /*de lire* in order to convey the momentous stimulation, excitation, and creative response a woman experiences when reading the text of another woman. The first section of *Amantes* includes multiple citations from other women writers; the words of Mary Daly, Monique Wittig, Sande Zeig, Michèle Causse, Adrienne Rich, Louky Bersianik, Djuna Barnes, and others designated by initials, are honoured by the refrain, "JE N'ARRÊTE PAS DE LIRE." The section following makes explicit the productive response provoked by a lover's text; it is a letter of straying response, a writing, which never abandons the imperative of reading: "si j'écris aujourd'hui, c'est afin de te lire mieux comme une provocation" (18), insists the speaker ["if i am writing today it is so i can read you better provocatively" (24)]. The process celebrated here is not a progression from reading to writing but an energizing circuit of mutual ignition.

Emergent in the poetic models of both Brossard and Godard is a network of agents – translator, reader, writer – all engaged in the production of text. For all, these roles are shared attentions, so that Godard's translating Brossard's book, the poet responding to her lover's letter, our reading the work, all these acts entail at some level reading, writing, translation. All entail refusing the single function, exploding the single meaning, stepping out of the straight furrow, deliring. Exploring the generative interconnectedness of these functions has been a lasting passion for Brossard, who declares, "I like to work with translators because it keeps me alert in my own language" (Williamson 71). *Le désert mauve [Mauve Desert]* explicitly demonstrates the interdependence of translation, reading, and writing. The deliring figure in this poetic novel is Maude Laures, who comes across Laure Angstelle's novel, <u>Le désert mauve</u> (comprising the first part of Brossard's book) in a second-hand bookstore; reading it, she is seduced into rewriting it, translating it into <u>Mauve L'Horizon</u> (comprising the last section of Brossard's book). Brossard collaborated with Daphne Marlatt on the mutual translations *Mauve* and *Character/Jeu de lettres*, poems replete with the energy produced when reading inflects translation inflects writing. The compositional processes here can be suggestively articulated through the invocation of a mode of interpretation Julia Kristeva names *delirium* (*délire* in the original French). After contextualizing Kristeva's *delirium* within the European tradition of thought around *délire* I will introduce her provocative notion into my discussion of the several acts of passage at work in the production of *Mauve Desert*, *Mauve* and *Character/Jeu de lettres*.

Délire, or *delirium* – Jean-Jacques Lecercle favours retaining the French in his discussion of this complex term – is a prevalent concept in European (particularly French) philosophy, linguistics and psychoanalysis. Lecercle's *Philosophy Through the Looking Glass* traces the various traditions and incarnations of *délire*, arriving at some definitions which are as consistent as such a critical text, which adopts a method informed by its own delirious object, can allow. Focussing on certain disjunctive writers (Roussel, Brisset, Wolfson), case-studies of schizophrenia (notably that of Daniel Paul Schreber) and unconventional critics (Gilles Deleuze), Lecercle characterizes *délire* as "a form of discourse [...] where the material side of language, its origin in the human body and *desire*, are no longer eclipsed by its abstract aspect (as an instrument of communication or expression)" (6). *Délire* is consistently referred to in Lecercle as "the other side of language" (65), a phrase which suggests this discursive mode's deviations from protocols of syntax, grammar, phonotactics, logic. Attending the uncertain distinction in Lecercle between the poet and the schizophrenic patient is a contradiction through which the issue of agency, or mastery, percolates. On the one hand Lecercle submits that "*délire* is a perversion which consists in interfering, or rather taking risks, with language" (16); he can also assert, however, that "in the case of *délire*, language is master" (9). Perhaps such an uncertainty surrounding the question of how the subject is disposed to language springs from Lecercle's notion (borrowed from Deleuze) that "*délire* is the linguistic manifestation of desire" (165). Desire can always be imagined, produced, theorized in complex, oblique and contradictory relation with the subject; we speak of desire as an unconscious drive, a conscious motivation and, indeed, a consciousness.[1] Consonant with Lecercle's ambivalence, Kristeva's delirious subject hovers over a distinction between being overwhelmed by the discursive mode of *délire* and employing it as a vehicle of transgression. Her important departure within a psychoanalytic tradition, however, lies in her refusal to reserve delirium for certain types of subjects, a refusal to fantasize, in other words, delirium as proper only to schizophrenic patients.

In "Psychoanalysis and the Polis," Kristeva argues that an interpreter should submit to the undeniable and exciting fact that "the knowing subject is also a *desiring* subject, and the paths of desire ensnarl the paths of knowledge" (307). The desire propelling Maude Laures's reading of <u>Mauve Desert</u> is made explicit. When that book falls into her hands it arouses "le lancinant désir qui ne la quittait pas" (55) ["the throbbing desire that never quit her" (51)]. While she has been "séduite" (66) ["seduced" (62)] by <u>Mauve Desert,</u> it is her own desire which extends the production of that book. The erotics thematized here points to a dynamic of intersubjectivity where the reader makes as many passes as there are passages. "Ensnarled" with desire, the reader's knowledge is subject to desire's unconscious realms, its changeability, vagaries, idio-syncrasies. Knowledge, giving way to delirium, proves neither a passive replica of its object nor the inevitable result of a predetermined interpretive schema which evacuates its object of possibility. What the delirious reader produces instead, Kristeva suggests, is "a fiction, an uncentred discourse, a subjective polytopia" (306). Certainly this is the outcome of Maude Laure's desir-ing, deliring interpretation as she writes her own deliri-ous "fiction," <u>Mauve the Horizon</u>. Differences attract my attention in *Mauve Desert*, in spite of – perhaps because of – the homolinguistic transfer enacted here. Shifts in phrasing, in stress, in mood, gentle and slick, in concert with moments when the translation leans in close to the source, produce a dynamic of fluid exchange. The fluidity here contradicts the popular translation strategy of *fluency*, in which the target text ideally appears as original. Fluent strategy erases signs of difference, performing a radical acculturation with an end to promoting the concept of universality (Venuti 1992, 5).   Feminist translator Susanne de Lotbinière-Harwood states that French language writ-ers enjoy the way her works

> retain a French 'accent,' making the new text foreign and familiar at the same time. This doubleness makes target-language readers aware that they are reading a translation by constantly putting them in the presence of otherness (150).

The chapbooks *Mauve* and *Character/ Jeu de lettres* display such an insistence on fluidity over fluency. Marlatt's poem "Character," includes a number of words in French or with French etymologies – "confrères," "personage," "finesse," "indissoluble" – exhibiting the interlingual exchange always already in motion and also risking initiative, making a first move, delivering the Barthesian fantasy of a text which desires its reader. She performs resistance to fluency in "Mauve/ A Reading," when she translates Brossard's "au bord de la mer" as "at the seabord." Most commonly, "au bord de la mer" would be interpreted as "at the seashore," but Marlatt chooses "seabord" in order to edge a little closer. In a gesture of what Lawrence Venuti would call "ethnodeviant translation" (1993, 210), she drops the *a* from the English *board*, committing an error in English spelling for the sake of a lingering "French Kiss."

Brossard makes a similar move with "come une ride de pluie"; *come* has lost its second *m* in translation, so while phonetically it signifies the French *comme* (like) it looks suspiciously like (*comme*) *come*, the English word for orgasm. And then there's *brandon*, a rare French word Brossard found to resonate with "branding." Carrying over the English *brand* marks a semantic gap, and an exceptional gift, as the primary meaning given for *brandon* is "trouble-maker," confirming

Brossard's declaration in "Poetic Politics" that her "'basic intention' [is] to make trouble, to be a trouble-maker in regard to language" (77). What some would identify as errors, Brossard celebrates as "trouble-making," a desire to intervene in a language compromised by the sedimentation of misogynist bias. And why shouldn't error be a place of possibility, horizon, since, as Marlatt suggests, language "misrepresents" us (1984, 55). The persistence of the improper at the edge, *at the seabord*, admits the potential for transformation.

Translator Susan Knutson has noted "I tend to err in the direction of meanings I desire" (1989, 16). Errors could be seen to result from the desire innervating delirium, a state in which, Kristeva says, "the speaking subject is presumed to have known an object, a relationship, an experience that he is henceforth incapable of reconstituting accurately" (307). The sense of *delire* as *err* and the idea of accuracy as casualty of desire raise questions about the role of voluntarism, or conscious rebellion, questions which Brossard engages in *Mauve Desert*. Close to the beginning of <u>A Book to Translate</u>, the elaborate 'between' of Brossard's book, appears the phrase, "Elle plonge, est-ce erreur ou stratégie" (57) ["She dives in, is this mistake or strategy" (53)]. Further down the page we find a word which might have occasioned that question, *l'auteure*. In French *auteur/author*, is gendered male; Brossard's erroneous addition of an *e muet*, or silent *e*, which marks the feminine in French grammar, makes visible the exclusionary function of grammatical structures and mobilizes the *e muet* with a view to feminist resignification.[2] The author is embodied differently through a mistake in spelling which has been foreshadowed as strategic. The inaccurate reconstitution of *auteur*, one that has been widely deployed by Quebec feminists, is indeed a grammatical error, yet an intentional one, one that attempts to makes sense of "the non-sense patriarchal reality constitutes for us" (*AL* 112).

When Susanne de Lotbinière-Harwood embarked on the English translation of *Le désert mauve*, she was faced with the dilemma of how to feminize *author* in a target language framed by different grammatical schemata. Feminist translators are aware that because of the "technical difficulties" between the two languages, English translations can neutralize feminist subversions which exploit the gender-marking of French. The force of error in its more delirious guise is evidenced in de Lotbinière-Harwood's anecdote about her translation of *auteure*:

> How it came about: my colleague Marie-Cécile Brasseur and I were drafting a work- related letter on computer. She was inputting as I dictated. Instead of typing 'author' she slipped and wrote 'auther.' "Eureka," I gasped, "that's it!" (131).

This instance of rebellion (which repeats with change both *auteure* and *author*) illustrates the potential of the cleavage in the subject discovered by psychoanalysis. Brasseur's "slip" is apparently unconscious yet consonant with the desires of a feminist poetic to the extent that Brasseur's collaborator, de Lotbinière-Harwood, regards it as a gift and a textual solution, reading into it and holding on to it strategically. Delirium, that state in which "the imaginary may join interpretive closure" (Kristeva 307), produces such gifts. More important than the quest to distinguish between the strategic and the erratic (and their respective value) is perhaps the ability to welcome moments when, in the rapturous state of delirium, the two are productively interlined.

The complex *auteure/auther* is the result of collaboration, not only between Brasseur and de Lotbinière-Harwood, but between de Lotbinière-Harwood and Brossard. The reader/translator's desire to find a feminized *author* is excited by Brossard's subversion, but that subversion is also extended through translation. Pertinent here is a description of the generative bivalence Kristeva observes in delirium:

> [...] the object may reveal to the interpreter the unknown of his theory and permit the constitution of a new theory. Discourse in this case is renewed; it can begin again: it forms a new object and a new interpretation in this reciprocal transference (306).

"Reciprocal transference" could serve to characterize the acts of passage carried out among the various readers/writers/translators I've been discussing. Replacing a notion of the unidirectional flow of knowledge (from intending author, from source language, from origi-

nal), delirium's "reciprocal transference" acknowledges the traffic between readers, languages, versions,
words. In <u>Mauve Desert</u>, the fictional author Laure
Angstelle writes, "Lorna dit qu'elle aimait le moly et la
mousse de saumon" (12) ["Lorna said she liked moly
and salmon mousse" (12)]. Noting the turbine of alliteration here, Maude Laures translates, "Lorna s'émer-
veilla à propos de la mousse au sommet des mon-
tagnes, douce sur les mollets" (182), moving *m*'s off of
the kitchen range and onto a mountain range. This is
truly "literal," letteral translation.[3] "Mousse" has survived the transfer physically intact, yet semantically
skewed, or expanded; the second *mousse* whips moss
into its antecedent, salmon mousse, conferring on it the
pleasure of a homonym. A further instance of reciprocal transference is inaugurated by de Lotbinière-
Harwood, when she reads Maude Laures's translation
as, "Lorna marveled over the moss on the mountain-
tops, soft against the shins" (168). Although "douce sur
les mollets" means "soft against the calves," de
Lotbinière-Harwood delires it as "soft against the
shins"; in doing so she welcomes the alliteration of the
original's *m*'s and *s*'s while moving meaning beyond.
Given a leg up, she twists it around for the sound of it,
for a new sense. Here is a moment which demonstrates
Lecercle's notion of *délire* as exposing "the material
side of language, its origin in the human body."

If absolute semantic propriety were the ideal, then
machine translation could have replaced the body of

the translator. In *Mauve* and *Character/ Jeu de lettres*, a kind of visual and aural fidelity moves in, an attentiveness to the physique of words. A sensual slant is crucial when the source text in question is experimental itself, engaged intently with the materiality of language. Marlatt moves "les liens autour de l'évidence" into "chained leans on the evidence." Nudging the meaning of 'links' over into the word "chained," she is able to respond to "liens" with the assonant "leans." When Brossard translates "liable" as "fiable," she risks semantic error in order to present a couple that look alike. Similarly, she maintains fidelity to play and music when she reads "S does not belong, goes beyond," as "L n'a de dieu, n'a de lieu." These lines arise out of Marlatt's poem around 'S' which returns as Brossard's poem around 'L', a shift occasioning the translation of the alliterative "signor, sister, son, sire, soprano" into "sibylle si belle elfe ellipse, la lyre." Brossard takes Marlatt's focus on the *S* as feminine signifier in "s/he:/ s plural in excess of he," and carries it into French as "i/lle: / l plurielles dans l'excès de ce qu'il."

The gap between *S* and *L* in the above poems points to the dimension of cultural specificity in feminist strategy. For feminist poets, the most significant linguistic difference between French and English is probably that of gender-marking. While entire signifying chains must, in French, be in gendered *agreement*, English is ostensibly more neutral. De Lotbinière-Harwood has made the provocative suggestion that this difference explains why "American feminists, whose thinking is couched in the seemingly more egalitarian and democratic English language have been striving for equality, while French feminist thinking has been articulated around sexual *différence*" (114). Brossard translates "character" as "genre" (gender) twice in "Jeu de Lettres," inflecting neutrality with a demand for the particular. Marlatt's section entitled «a mark» and Brossard's response, «signature», illustrate the tension between idiom-specific strategies:

«a mark»	«signature»
born in name, I the undersigned	née dans le nom, je soussignée
established character, given the	dans le genre établi, compte tenu
references of friends, confreres in	des références d'amis, confrères
business, credit on tap, sign	en affaire, signe à crédit
this personage	ce personage
a person portrayed	une personne décrite
by himself	en son portrait à l'écart

Marlatt's version plays on the neutrality of English, invoking terms like "character," "personage," and "person," which are technically inclusive. By ending the poem with "by himself," however, she underscores the fact that English is not so terribly neutral; this is a language where *he*, *man* and *himself* are posited as comprehensive, fostering the assumption that "character," "personage" and "person" are male until proven otherwise. "Confreres," appearing in the middle of the poem, quietly anticipates Marlatt's cadential revelation of a subsuming "he/man"[4] language. In Brossard's version, on the other hand, "confreres" sticks out, a gender-marked term differing from the speaking subject, who is clearly marked as feminine from the beginning by the *e muet* in "née" and "soussignée." While «a mark» exposes the erasure inhering in neutrality, «signature» is propelled through energies of incongruity. It is perhaps the presentation of these French and English poems together which represents the most generative feminist strategy. The visibility of translation, the effect, for example, of the irresolution between marked and unmarked proposes an environment of linguistic flux and possibility.

Mauve and *Character/Jeu de lettres* are instances of feminist creative translation in which transfer occurs not only interlingually, but intralingually also, as each poet works at subverting the androcentrism of her own language. The latter engine is the one propelling Brossard's *Mauve Desert*. While this novel's pretense of dual authership offers a crucial critique of conventional notions of originality and translative invisibility, as well as dramatizing the energy and erotics made possible through the textual meeting of two women, *Mauve Desert* is, of course, written by Brossard. This novel is a more theatrical incarnation of a compositional process Brossard engages in all her writing, a delirous self-reading, a poetics of autotranslation. In "Reading Nicole Brossard," Susam Knutson articulates the dynamic function of translation in Brossard's poetic:

> As in *L'Aviva*, Brossard in *Le Désert mauve* translates Brossard from French into French, and again, she points clearly to translation not so much as an exploration of the physical frontiers of languages and cultures – although these are still present as fictions, as metaphors, as incitations – but rather as the drive to reach the internal horizons of meaning and the consciousness or construction of reality (12).

While I would use the term metonym, rather than metaphor, to characterize translation's intimate relation to her poetics – thus my inclusion of the Marlatt, Godard and de Lotbinière-Harwood material – I take as paramount Knutson's observation that it is the "internal horizons" which are at stake. Internal horizons comprise the field of action in a translative poetic; one writer reads her own text over, looking behind and ahead of words, so that language chafes at itself and at the realities it both reflects and envisions. Extending the bounds of translation proper, Brossard's practice ranges from the introversion of the intralingual to the radically collaborative, sustaining always the critique, friction, dream and renewal of *délire*.

Notes

1. Lesbian performance artist Holly Hughes recalls discovering her desire as an experience "that the expression 'coming out' doesn't quite cover. In my case, it was more a question of [...] coming to' (191).

2. An early, if not the first, instance of the transgressive, feminist e muet appears in the

title of Brossard's 1974 collection *Mécanique jongleuse, suivi de Masculin gram-maticale,* a work infused with the force of women's desire and of that desire's vol-canic effect on language.

3. My use of literal here favors the Oxford dictionary definition, "expressed by letters of the alphabet." Louis and Celia Zukofsky's translation of Catullus is founded on this definition, as their preface indicates: "This translation of Catullus follows the sound, rhythm, and syntax of his Latin – tries, as is said, to breathe the 'liter-al' meaning with him" (unpag.).

4. I take this term from Dale Spender's *Man Made Language.* See her chapter "Language and Reality: Who Made the World?" for an analysis of the ways English grammar has been systematically shaped to reinforce notions of male superiority.

Works Cited

Hughes, Holly. "Clit Notes." *Clit Notes: A Sapphic Sampler*. New York: Grove Press, 1996.

Knutson, Susan. "Reading Nicole Brossard." *Ellipse*. 53 (1995): 9-21.

——, with K. Mezei, D. Marlatt, B. Godard, G. Scott. "Vers-ions con-verse: A Sequence of Translations." *Tessera* 6 (1989): 16-23.

Kristeva, Julia. "Psychoanalysis and the Polis." *The Kristeva Reader*. Trans. Margaret Waller. Ed. Toril Moi. New York: Columbia U P, 1986. 301-320.

Lecercle, Jean-Jacques. *Philosophy Through the Looking Glass: Language, nonsense, desire*. La Salle, Ill.: Open Court, 1985.

Lotbinière-Harwood, Susanne de. *Re-Belle et Infidèle/ The Body Bilingual*. Montréal and Toronto: Les Éditions du Remue-Ménage/ Women's Press, 1991.

Marlatt, Daphne. "musing with mothertongue." *Tessera/ Room of One's Own* 8 (1984): 53-56.

Marlatt, Daphne and Nicole Brossard. *Character/ Jeu de lettres*. Montréal: Nouvelle Barre du Jour/Writing, 1986.

Spender, Dale. *Man Made Language*. London: Routledge and Kegan Paul, 1980.

Venuti, Lawrence, ed. *Rethinking Translation: Discourse, Subjectivity, Ideology*. London and New York: Routledge, 1992.

——. "Translation as cultural politics: regimes of domestication in English." *Textual Practice*. 7.2 (1993): 208-23.

Williamson, Janice. Interview with Nicole Brossard. *Sounding Differences: Conversations with Seventeen Canadian Women Writers*. Toronto: U of Toronto P, 1993. 57-74.

Zukofsky, L. and Zukofsky, C. *Catullus (Gai Catulli Veronensis Liber)*. London: Cape Goliard Press, and New York: Grossman, 1969.

Life (in) Writing

Or a Writing-Machine for Producing the Subject

Barbara Godard

Alors je me suis demandé s'il y avait un rapport entre la Martinique, la mort et le fait d'aller au paradis (JI 37)
[Then I wondered whether there was any relation between Martinique, death and going to paradise.]

Journaling is popularly recommended as a way to master time's inexorable flux and consolidate a coherent self. Temporality, writing, and the subject are indeed Nicole Brossard's concerns in *Journal intime*.[1] With a difference, however – that puzzling *relation* in my epigraph – which interrogates all representational practices with their logic of separation and substitution in the play of absence/presence of referential illusion. For as *Journal intime* self-reflexively proclaims, it is an *optical illusion*, a fictive text "qui n'en finit plus de [susciter] toutes les questions qu'on peut imaginer" (61) ["that [stirs up] all the questions one could possibly imagine"]. Among these questions, the one I shall pursue here is how to create a device for conveying the fine, shifting line between fiction and reality as Brossard explores ways in which material gestures generate utopian possibilities. Writing and memory become irrevocably intertwined, creating an archive of texts and affects, one that seizes upon a moment of visceral sensation to recognize the past in its becomings.

In an epigraph to *Journal intime*, Brossard quotes Sartre on diary writing: "pour tenir un journal, il faut n'avoir rien à faire donc rien à dire" (11) ["to keep a journal, you must have nothing to do and so nothing to say"]. This quote introduces a series of citations from the works of famous writers that self-reflexively address the vertiginous abyss between sensation and notation that haunts any project of life-writing. The journal, a way of killing time, of filling a void, nonetheless consumes time and monumentalizes it so that nothing remains except the obsession of writing in which one loses oneself in the "sounds of the fury of writing," as Brossard allusively puns. "«Elle vivait de mots», dira-t-on un jour" (33) ["'She lived on words', they'll say one day"]. Sartre's phrase pithily formulates the dilemma faced by all writers since Flaubert announced his project to write a book about nothing and produced one composed entirely of presumed clichés. In this representational paradox, there is nothing outside signification: a word does not stand for a thing but, self-reflexively, connotes its position within a linguistic system. The contradiction of absence as transcendence weighs heavily on the subject which, according to Benveniste, is an effect of the speech act – of the performative – involving the personal pronoun and the copula verb, a shifter or empty signifier, linked reciprocally to each speaker in turn. In this recursive process, under the burden of such a mobile signifier, the subject flounders, incapacitated by the attempt to synthesize its proliferations and, tautological, turns around and around on itself to the point of exhaustion. "C'est, par le vide" ["In the void"], as Brossard notes, "le sujet mis hors de combat" (9) ["the subject is sidelined from action"]. In the dominant Western theorization of the subject, Brossard contends, the subject resides in a congestion of signifiers and overwhelming emotions, discernable only as comparison through the power of metaphor.

Exhaustion, however, is not how Brossard regards such dispersion. "La survie du sujet est tridimensionnelle" ["The subject survives three-dimensional"] in its many lives and modes of sensation and consciousness that "tradui[sent] notre expérience du réel" (9-10) ["translate our experience of reality"]. But how to get beyond the binaries of the dominant, masculinist symbolic order? Dispersion is certainly not considered the *end of history*. Receptivity to it offers promise of a new form for the story, rather, one not without affinities to Gertrude Stein's cubist experiments in portraiture as an affair of composition. Brossard's *These Our Mothers* ends with a vision of history in "la forme des femmes dans la trajectoire de l'espèce" (*A* 99) ["the form of women organizing in the trajectory of the species" (*TM* 101)]. And a concern with *succession* or genealogy is of central concern in *Journal intime*, emerging as an explicit preoccupation in the second edition of the text with the linkage of the reflection upon "ces images de femmes gravides qui sillonnent l'histoire de l'art et de la représentation" (92) ["the succession of pregnant women throughout the history of art and representation"] to the maternal genealogy of four women in the context of the historical crises of the twentieth century (109). Here the relation of art to life is approached through the figure of metonymy and relations of contingency and combination, rather than metaphor's operations of resemblance and substitution. *Oeuvre de Chair [Works in Flesh]* is Brossard's title for this sequence of metonymies introduced into the second edition of *Journal intime*. Like such feminist theorists as Hélène Cixous and Luce Irigaray, Brossard has challenged a history of figuration of the feminine as vanishing point in Western philosophical discourse to read this gap or hollow through a different frame of desire as a space of becomings.

Whereas in his revolutionary novel *Prochain épisode* Hubert Aquin, celebrated Québec writer of the *nouveau roman*, focusses on the necessity of overcoming ambiguity in the closure of death, Brossard ripostes with a text about fiction's transformative power entitled *She Would Be the First Sentence of My Next Novel* that conveys anticipation in such uncertainty, the productive possibility of the wavering moment of indecision. Aquin's novel comes to an end with the lines, "Yes, that is the conclusion to the story: because everything has an end. I shall go to meet the woman who's still waiting for me on the terrace of the Hôtel d'Angleterre. That's what I'll say in the final sentence of my novel. And a few lines later. I shall write in capital letters the words: THE END" (123).

In *Journal intime* Brossard quotes the opening phrase of *Prochain épisode*, along with the *incipit* of novels by Camus and Ducharme that begin with the death of the mother and a movement of being overwhelmed by everything, only to consign such fictional gestures to the past, as her litany of *yesterdays* framing them makes explicit. Like Clarice Lispector, whom she also cites at this juncture, "I'm almost free of my mistakes" (*Stream* 12). Whereas *Journal intime*, working through the archive and memory, looks backward to interrogate the fictional canon, *She Would Be the First Sentence*, engaging with the utopian dreams of alternative potential, luxuriates in the hesitation of beginnings. As the *persona* announces: "Elle aimait cet état précurseur de dimension nouvelle, état qui la rendait vulnérable mais qui toujours s'affirmait comme un signe d'espoir" ["She loved this state signalling a new dimension, this state that made her vulnerable but asserted itself always as a sign of hope" (6, 7)]. The text begins in the past, then shifts quickly into the conditional, into the *as if*, fictional tense *par excellence*, as it tackles the hitherto *undecipherable*:

Il y avait maintenant plus d'un an qu'elle songeait à son

prochain roman. Le roman s'organiserait autour de ce qui, maintenant énigmatique en elle, se déploierait dans quelques mois majestueusement comme une longue métaphore de vie ou cruellement au rythme de la conscience qui ne laisserait rien au hasard (6).

She had been thinking about her next novel for over a year. The novel would take shape around that which, though presently enigmatic insider her, would unfold in a few months, majestically like a long metaphor of life or cruelly, to the rhythm of consciousness that would leave nothing to chance (7).

This first passage ends with the observation that the *persona* will be concerned less with enumerating story elements than with tracing narrative transformations from the point of impact of contradictory energies. Focussing on processes, not bounded entities or fixed states, Brossard avoids a new ontology and so transforms the models of knowing and identity. Even in the final lines of *She Would Be the First Sentence*, the *persona* "pense à mon prochain roman" [is still "thinking about my next novel"], "l'imagine quelque mots plus loin, quelques mois plus tard" [still "imagining her a few words farther on, a few months later"], possibly finishing up her lecture, yet reflecting nonetheless on the future *consequences* of writing "*je suis une femme*" (142) ["*I am a woman*" (143)].

The complex temporality of the future perfect is compounded in this last sentence which figures prominently in the opening section of *These Our Mothers*, written more than twenty years earlier. Circling back to the first of Brossard's feminist fictions, this quoted phrase functions here as a "relais de ferveur" (*NV* 13) ["fervent relay" (*GN* 29)] or image that forges strange connections, establishing relations of effective and affective change. Quotations of texts are rewritten into a new contextual web of signification that injects a different energy, a different intensity. In revitalizing the fragments, the text transforms a culture of death into one of life.

Brossard has long pursued an investigation into the possibilities opened up by language's self- referentiality after she realized that, if a word did not refer to one thing, it could evoke many things in its potential combinations of signifiers within a network of other signs. Since the suite of poems *Le centre blanc* (1970), constructed on a series of words – muscle, energy, desire, death, negated through the paradoxical meanings of *personne* (which contradictorally means both somebody and no-one, this person, this language, which is not one) – her writing has focussed on the white page and the energy of the mind contemplating its own processes of thought, the consciousness of self-consciousness. Such thought experiments constitute one way of in(ter)venting the real. Reality, as she observes in *La lettre aérienne*, is a fiction or figure of the imagination imposed by power that arbitrates the border between what it is possible to say and what remains unspeakable. Fictions currently taken for the real are those of

"l'appareil militaire, la montée du prix de l'or" ["military apparatus, the rise in the price of gold"], while
many *realities* of women's everyday life such as "la
maternité, le viol, la prostitution, la fatigue chronique,
la violence subie (verbale, physique et mentale)" (53)
["maternity, rape, prostitution, chronic fatigue, verbal,
physical, and mental violence" (75)] are published in
the newsmedia as stories, not fact. Presented as
women's words, however, and put on the page, such
memories become *fiction-theory*, fiction deployed as
thought experiment or hypothesis ("if... then") to
rework the social imaginary or as a writing-machine
producing forms to "Résoudre des problèmes de sens"
["resolve problems of sense"] and "rend[re la réalité]
sujette à transformation" (144) ["subject" reality "to
transformation" (149)]. Such *intercepting the real* is
performed through language and its images or figures
in their function as *relays* or *transmission devices*. The
dynamic linkages render reality proximate and so facilitate transference, with a consequent transformation in
consciousness and motivation.

Since the publication of *Un livre*, Brossard has
increasingly written *fiction-theory* in order to shift our
perceptions and make a "brèche" ["breach"] or "rupture" in what we understand as reality (*LA* 59/ *AL* 81).
Throughout the 1970s her *writing as research* focussed
on the processes of perception, emphasizing in particular the materiality of the book and the embodied reading of graphic notation or textual *skin*. Her play with

typography draws attention to the *surfaces of sense* as both sensory and mental apprehension. Language does not reflect any pre-existent entity but *makes sense*. The work of this decade culminated in *Le sens apparent [Surfaces of Sense]*, which thematized these concerns with the material properties of language to create an effect of the real. Situated within the "spirale dans les livres écrits par des femmes" (14) ["spiral pattern in books written by women" (14)], it reworks fragments from other women's texts into a different context in which the various authors and their characters take on a life as characters in a new fictional universe and so embody Brossard's interest in realizing "les versions" (76) ["all the versions" (74)] or potentials of an utterance. In particular, her concern has been to intervene in the symbolic economies of patriarchy that have constituted the feminine as lack, as mere token of exchange, in order to hypothesize an alternate economy in which women will engage in relations of equitable exchange with other women. No longer a relation of subject to object, reading and rewriting the texts produced by other women constitute an intersubjective exchange in *Surfaces of Sense* which, in another twist to the spiral, returns to rework the issues raised in two of Brossard's earlier texts. *These Our Mothers* stages a violent assault on the patriarchal order to kill its symbolic mother and write the feminine into history, while *Lovhers*, in dialogue with the love poems of Adrienne Rich, unfolds a story of the production and reading of the text with the frame of a love letter to another woman. It concludes with an eloquent evocation of the spiral as a utopian continent peopled by lesbian writers. This play of allusion unbinds the text in an emphasis on the unlimited play of difference. While *Lovhers* explores the emotion of thought, and *These Our Mothers* the thought of emotion, *Surfaces of Sense* examines the sensation of thought and emotion through the figure of the *skin* of the text where these two sources of information are intimately intertwined in *surfaces of sense*.

In the 1990s Brossard was less concerned with shaping the emergence of a collective memory to transform our relation to the present than she was in exploiting fiction's temporal play to make possible worlds in the future. *She Would Be the First Sentence of My Next Novel* manifests most powerfully Brossard's persistent desire to follow the trace of thought with microscopic attention, in this case through the operation of the conditional tense. *Baroque at Dawn*, her other major fiction of the decade, explores the intimate connection between fiction and futurity through multiple modes of representation, in particular the older forms of photography and writing, as well as recent digital forms of virtual reality. Such virtuality creates a present that "s'éternis[e]" (176) [that is "never-ending" (172)], a present of potentiality for actualization. As the character Cybil Noland writes near the conclusion of the novel, "qui invente autrui sait que c'est toujours devant soi" (227) ["one who invents someone else knows the other will always be up there ahead" (223)] in the curvature of the baroque fold or the fractal. "Nous ne savons pas comment arrêter de penser futur" (242) ["We can't stop thinking future (238)], yet "Le futur nous enracine dans la fiction" (229) ["The future roots us in fiction" (225)] recursively. Along with the mobility of language, fiction brings a superposition of clashing perspectives, "Ramification sans fin ouverture" (253) ["Ramification without end, a new opening" (249)]. Such "random mingling" of disparate entities – the collision of languages (Spanish/English/French), cultures (Argentina/U.K./Québec), genders (lesbian/ heterosexual) – creates energy and excitement that jolts us and awakens our "aptitude au voyage" (229) [sets us "voyaging" (225)]. In order to promote radical transformation, then, "Il fallait tourner la langue vers le futur" (142) ["Language must be turned toward the future" (136)] and diversify through disjunctive syntheses as "La réalité se superpos[e] à la réalité" (174) ["Reality superpose[s] itself on reality" (170)] in rhizomatic becoming.

As in her other works of *fiction-theory*, in *Baroque at Dawn* Brossard juxtaposes prose poems with fragments of narrative exposition and passages of formal and erudite language with colloquial speech, or with invented words, in an aesthetic of the disjunctive fragment. These structural features contribute to the vertiginous perspectival and temporal play between the virtual and the actual – between the author Brossard, a Québécoise, the character Nicole Brossard, who is an *English* novelist, and the character Cybil Noland, another anglophone novelist. Meeting the character Brossard at a conference on autobiography, Noland comments on the absurdity of "wanting to enter into the world of fiction while remaining oneself." This is the principal paradox of all Brossard's writing, most prominently of *Journal intime* where Brossard of 1983 meets many other Brossards. In an additional moment of "exubérance baroque" (*BA* 249) ["baroque exuberance" (*BD* 245)], one of Noland's novels is being translated into French, and she is involved in dialogues with the translator in a veritable "sensation du double présent" (84) ["double-present sensation" (76)]. These dialogues playfully recite and resite the desire for a dialogue with the author Laure Angstelle that animates Maude Laure's project of translation in *Mauve Desert*. They restage in the mode of fiction the dialogue between Brossard and her critic, Louise Forsyth, and translator, Barbara Godard, that forms the recording of the *life (in) writing* in *Journal intime*. Among other such doublings in *Baroque at Dawn* the lesbian lovemaking of the opening section folds the eroticism of Brossard's first book, *Aube à la saison,* published thirty years earlier, into a different sexual economy, which unfolds in the central section, "Le futur *dark*" ["The *Dark* Future"], onto a dystopic virtual reality in which women serve as objects for the pornographic gaze of

heterosexuality. Time is conceived as a rupture contin-
uously opened between the multiplication of the visible, the beautiful, and the barbarity of its hidden side,
in what Christine Buci-Glucksmann calls "baroque
reason" with its logic of contradiction (not analogy)
and its mathematics of the curve or the fold – fold
upon fold upon fold.

While the association of this perspectival play with
the baroque marks a difference in Brossard's conceptu-
alization of her project today, the formal doubling and
explicit link in technologies of the virtual extend and
thematize what was implicit in her writing throughout
the 1980s, namely its concern with repetition and signification. Does the gap between versions result in loss
or potential? Translation, long Brossard's major figure
for thinking repetition with a difference in her earlier
writing, is further explored in *Baroque at Dawn*
through the figure of the fold with its continuous vari-
ation. Translation is no longer the terrain of the melan-
cholic condemned to senseless repetition in an oedipal-
ized economy of loss and gain, but is conceptualized as
excess in the multiple potentials for renewal it generates. Opening to a new horizon, directing another light
onto the scene of violent loss, translation promises to
yield new works of art and new loves.

Obliquely here, I've been tracing the movement of
Mauve Desert through the changes produced by a trans-
position of the narrative from the lurid light rupturing
the night of the Nevada desert, site of nuclear and

other explosions, to the hopeful emotions under the
cool northern light where Maude Laures performs an
intralinguistic translation of Laure Angstelle's fiction
and renders it as <u>Mauve, the Horizon</u>. Maude inter-
venes subtly in her translation to change the intensity,
the rhythm and the affective colouration of Angstelle's
narrative. Significantly, in her translation she shifts the
angle of perception from the dead Angela Parkin to
Melanie, the teenager dancing with Angela when she
was shot, and so modulates the narrative centre from a
speculative fiction about detection, focussed on death
from misogyny, to a utopian fiction about the power of
love between women to alter the course of a life, the
course of (hi)story. Maude rewrites the final pages of
the text to focus on Melanie: she comments on how,
when Melanie spoke, it awakened in Maude "the horizon" – an opening and renewal of possibilities. "Mais
la nuit" [but the night] yields to the new beginnings
ushered in with the dawn. Maude has resisted death as
an ending throughout the course of the narrative. Yet it
is only at the conclusion of the third version of the story
that she becomes involved with the living woman within the character. As Angela summarizes this transfor-
mational process: "il suffit de quelques mots concis
pour changer le cours de la mort" (220) ["a few concise
words are enough to change the course of death"
(201)]. In the centerfold of the book, "Un livre à
traduire" ["A Book to Translate"] – the fictional translator's narrative – Maude reveals how Angstelle's book

struck her as a flash of insight, compelling her to immerse herself in its world by repeating it through translation. So thoroughly does she enter the textual world that she identifies with the author to the point of fantasizing a dialogue with Angstelle where the positions of author and character, author and translator are at stake in Brossard's probing of the boundaries or limits of the writing subject and the transformative power of reading.

In its use of the book within the book and its extended passages of homolinguistic translation – Mauve, the Horizon repeats the entire first section, Mauve Desert, with a difference by using homonyms, synonyms, and punctuation changes – *Le désert mauve* explores most fully the strategies Brossard embraced throughout the 1980s, strategies that, with significant variations, shaped *Journal intime*. Although the fictional journal also relies on displacement through repetition as a strategy of modulation, its unit of repetition is primarily the word, rather than the phoneme, as in such intralinguistic translations as *L'aviva*, which uses the echo effect of syllable sounds to create new words with different meaning. In this, *Journal intime* has greater affinities with Brossard's meditation on the virtual and the actual in *Picture Theory*. Represented as a hologram, of which any part may actualize the potentialities of the whole, the final section of *Picture Theory* – Hologramme, presumably published in 2002 – is again a novel within the novel, a book within the book. <u>Hologramme</u> briefly recapitulates the entire narrative through its repetition of key words. And it is such a strategy that Brossard uses in *Journal intime* in each of the five sections where first the *posture* and then the poem select a few words from the various entries and recombine them in new juxtapositions that demonstrate the virtual potentials of language as a system to generate infinite meanings from a fixed number of letters.

Commissioned by Radio-Canada for a series of writers' diaries, *Journal intime* was written from 26 January to 28 March 1983 and read by Pol Pelletier in a broadcast series over a week in August of that year. Brossard worked with the constraints of such a format to denaturalize both writing and the construction of identity. Formal constraints are intensified with the subsequent addition of the postures and poems in the published version which foregrounds the shift in enunciative position from voice to writing. The formal investigation of representation as metaphor is subject to further interrogation in the second edition of *Journal intime* when *common sense* regarding representation is juxtaposed to alternate logics of relation in the metonymies of *Oeuvre en chair [Works in Flesh]*. Flaunting its fictionality, *Journal intime* violates the generic conventions of the journal, notably its immediate and informal record of a single day in a chronological sequence. Ironically, Brossard is reticent about personal details in all her texts, focussing more on the charged moments when the everyday breaks into the processes of reading to incite the associative flux of memory, as when returning on the bus from the funeral of a friend's mother, the *persona* reads in a novel about a funeral passing in the very street where she had lived as a child. This image in the fiction sets her adrift on the floods of memory, shifting abruptly from the red of a traffic light that catches her eye in passing to a memory of viewing petals on birds of paradise outside a church in Martinique. A "fervent relay," the image sets up lines of desire interrupting linearity. The sequence culminates in her meditation on the *relation* between death, paradise, and Martinique (*JI* 37) and the power of making such strained connections through the relay of language that enables her to live in the deferred temporality of the virtual, the present tense of writing, playing games with the reader's expectations of continuity as she "ruses with reality," and so opens the opportunity through writing for *changing the subject*.

Notes

1. All quotations from *Journal intime* are taken from the 1998 edition. I have done all translations; see my recently published translations, with *Introduction: Intimate Journal or Here's a Manuscript*, followed by *Works of Flesh and Metonymies*. This essay draws on some of my earlier writing about Brossard, especially "Producing Visibility for Lesbians: Nicole Brossard's Quantum Poetics" and "Anjos/Angulos: Da Tarefa Angelical Ao Traduzir da Mulher."

Works Cited

Aquin, Hubert. *Prochain épisode*. Trans. Penny Williams. Toronto: McClelland & Stewart, 1967. Trans. of Prochain épisode. Montréal: Le Cercle du Livre de France, 1965.

Camus, Albert. *The Stranger*. (1942). Trans. Matthew Ward. New York: Knopf, 1988.

Deleuze, Gilles. *The Logic of Sense*. (1969). Trans. Mark Lester with Charles Stivale. Ed. Constantin V. Boundas. New York: Columbia, 1990.

Ducharme, Réjean. *The Swallower Swallowed*. (1966). Trans. Barbara Bray. London: Hamish Hamilton, 1968.

Godard, Barbara. "Producing Visibility for Lesbians: Nicole Brossard' Quantum Poetics." English Studies in Canada 21.2 (1995): 125-137.

——. "Anjos/Angulos: Da Tarefa Angelical Ao Traduzir da Mulher" (English version 1993). Trans. Marilia Scaff. *Revista de estudios de literatura* 5 (otubro 1997): 155-180.

Irigaray, Luce. *Le corps-à-corps avec la mère*. Montreal: Les Éditions de la Pleine Lune, 1981.

Lispector, Clarice. *The Stream of Life*. Trans. Earl Fitz & Elizabeth Lowe. Minneapolis: U Minnesota Press, 1989. Trans. of Agua Viva. Rio de Janeiro: Editora Artenova, 1973

The *Inédit* in Writing by Nicole Brossard

Breathing the Skin of Language

LYNETTE HUNTER

In the necessity and the desire to reinvent the language there are certainly an intention of happiness, a utopic thread, a serious responsibility (WT 184).

I am interested in knowledge and moral action.[1] Hence I engage with Nicole Brossard's work mainly through her sense of language being the material place for the articulation of the unthought and unknown (one cannot know until a thing is articulated), which in itself is moral action. The unknown doesn't just get said. It's a laborious process of working on the words, a kind of training in engagement specific to each reader-writer relationship, that is coincident with the engagement itself. The better trained one is, the more material the engagement, to the point that the writer-reader begin to articulate together, to work on growing the skin of language, the huge second lung of breath on which the material depends. Yet training never stops. If it does, the articulation becomes representation, or reproduction in the Marxist sense, and language splits into the semantic and fictional divide about which Brossard speaks so often.

To get there is difficult. Brossard's criticism, like her

poetry from which it is scarcely distinguishable, uses words that are over-oxygenated because we often don't know how to take up the invitation to work on articulation. The critical text gives off energy at random, makes us vulnerable in the intimacy of conceptual sensation it promises, leaves me light-headed or feeling the unbearable intensity of insistent but elusive significance. I have to train to read so that the images do not drift toward nausea but toward meaning. I have to learn to work with the texts – but what makes me persist as I am flung from white space to white space? Probably the quite different experience of reading Brossard's novels in a classroom with a group of other readers, and I will return to *Baroque at Dawn* in the concluding discussion. But also, because my experience of reading Brossard's texts is so similar to her descriptions of writing them.

In "Au*ther*" Brossard reiterates a topic that infuses her writing of the late 1990s, and states that she is a humanist writer "profoundly moral, that is to say attentive to human life in its small and great struggles to signify beyond reproduction" (2). The definition is significant: unlike the ethical, which is bound to ideological and discursive institutions of power, the moral delineates our willingness to take into account all that representation ignores or obscures or represses, all the messy details of our lives that are beyond reproduction because they do not fit. To attend to the moral we have to work on articulating those parts of life/our lives that are not-yet-said, a process Brossard calls the *inédit*, which is fundamentally an exploration of the creation of knowledge. Her writing works endlessly on articulating and increasingly on what *articulating* is, how it happens. This is one of the most pressing philosophical issues of humanist inquiry and politics that we face today in western democratic states, because of the growing pressure of overdetermination by institutional power and new technologies operating on a global scale and denying located knowledge, agency and moral action to the individual. Yet there are remarkably few attempts to write about the *process of creation* that articulating involves, to bring into presence and recognition the material reality of the body and word of the *inédit*.

This essay charts a movement among the representative, the fictional and the material: the semantic, the installation and the *inédit* or articulation of the not-yet-said. Brossard speaks of this slightly differently in "Trajectory" when she describes the process of creation in writing as "a wager of presence in the semantic, imaginary and symbolic space" (179). This movement suggests that those locations are not fully distinct, but are particular and necessary to new developments in democratic humanism that distinguish it from the exclusionary rhetoric of liberal humanism that has dominated the formation of nation states in the west.

Installation: Desire and Discourse

A recent translation of *Installations (avec et sans pronoms)* clarifies an entire range of theoretical inquiry and cultural study in western liberal democracies. During the 1960s and early 1970s, neo-Marxist theory combined with Lacanian psychoanalysis to define individuals as 'subjects' when they participated in the ideological symbolic system of representation. As is well-known, the feminist response to these ideas which deny women subjecthood was to claim the pre-symbolic for itself, for women's consciousness did not enter the world of ideological representations in the same way, if at all, as men's. The feminist response facilitated and contributed to a much wider understanding that the symbolic system defined as Lacanian also denied subjecthood to people of colour, to the poor, to those of different ability and age – in effect to all those who were not part of the small group of propertied, white, Judaeo-Christian men who worked in and on institutions of power (see Hunter). But for all the hegemonic analysis of *subjectivity* or *subject position* as terms to define the activity of individuals not systemically part of hegemony yet contributing to its maintenance (much of which focussed around the work of M. Foucault after 1976, and the political theory of E. Laclau and C. Mouffe in the 1980s), there was little in

the growing field of discourse studies that could identify the agency of the individual and hence the field of
moral action.

Brossard's use and elaboration of *installation* is an
early and prescient development of the idea of "constituted" subject positions made by gender studies to discourse theory from the mid 1980s to the mid 1990s. To
name but one, Judith Butler's concept of "performance" as the activity of a "constituting subject" always
retained the emphasis on the hegemonic and ideological, simply because of the linguistic bond to the *subject*
defined by the Lacanian symbolic. *Installations,* by con-
trast, swings the weighting to the individual's ability to
"fictionalise": if we are denied participation as a *subject*,
yet recognise that subjectivity is a matter of representation rather than nature, then why not make our own
fictions?

In *Installations* the verse "Installation" presents the
writer settling "je m'installe dans mon corps / de
manière à pouvoir bouger / quand une femme me fait
signe" (47) ["into my body's installation / so as to be
able to respond / when a woman gives me a sign" (49).
On the opposite page is the verse "Ombre" ["Shadow"]
in which"une belle subjectivité" ["a beautiful subjectivity"] "n'entame pas / la lucidité" ["doesn't broach /
lucidity"] in which the body "prononce de l'ombre /
avide d'images" ["pronounce[s] shadow / avid for
images"] and in which we are left to "songer *ma vie* /
au bout des bras" (46) ["dream[ing] *my life* / at arm's

length" (48)]. All ideological representations are constructed from real material, from actual individuals. In order to fit representation, elements must be left out or hidden, so in a sense all representations that are allowed to subjects cast a shadow. Often characterised as *loss* or *absence*, this shadow is in effect just as material and actual, but without words, without visibility, unrecognised. And if the materiality *installs* itself, presents itself so that it can be recognised, it attains agency. Writing is one means by which we effect this installation for, as Brossard puts it in "Writing as a Trajectory of Desire and Consciousness" published a few years later but containing more contemporary material, writing "translates that enigmatic but reflective operation whereby we process and can transform our versions of reality, that is change its metaphoric and semantic course" (179).

The Inédit: Articulation of the not-yet-said – from Installation to the Body

Installations proceeds to some extent by probing the thresholds between shadow and installation, probing the possibilities for recognising the not-said, not-made-public emotions, feelings, events, significances in our lives. However, the next move toward agency is articulation of the recognised. First in that movement is the difficulty of identifying the not-said as not-yet-said, acknowledging that this is not a matter of lack or

absence but of material presence that can be articulated, and once articulated becomes knowledge that can
inform moral action. The exploration of the not-said
into the *inédit* emerges in many of Brossard's essays of
the late 1980s and into the 90s. By the time of "Fluid
Arguments" she is arguing that the production of the
inédit traverses all her books (316). One helpful work
from 1990, translated in 1997 along with *Typhon dru*, is
"Harmonious Matter Still Manoeuvres," which reiter-
atively explores the "not-yet-said" by saying it, and in
the process offers a series of remarkable articulations.

The first stanza suggests that a thought that arises
"au milieu de la réalité et de ses poses innommables"
["in the midst of reality, its unnameable poses"]
prompts her despite the *unnameable* to have recourse to
the thought that "rien n'est trop lent, ni trop bref pour
l'univers" ["nothing is too slow nor too brief for the
universe" (8/9)]. The second stanza claims "je sais que
tout n'est pas dit parce que mon corps s'est installé avec
un certain bonheur dans cette pensée" ["I know that all
isn't said because my body settles with a certain joy into
such a thought"].[2] This sends words into a trajectory
along which she can "en liant les voyelles et le dos des
pensées me rapprocher, les yeux bridés de fascination, de
la mort et de son contraire" ["by joining vowels and the
spine of thoughts, get closer, with eyes narrowed in fascination, to death and its opposite" (10-11, my translation)]. There is no clear *meaning* from this syntax (not-
sentence). There is resistant *signification*. Articulation is

not a solitary process and the reader must engage with the trajectory of words even to recognise them as writing any material presence let alone the materiality itself.

Each stanza in "Harmonious" presents a moment of possible recognition, a moment of words for the not-yet-said being thrown out in arcs whose movement we may recognise and engage with, or not. Whether we do so is largely a matter of training in word skills – the techniques, strategies and stances of poetic and rhetoric – and a willingness to take up the politics of reading. Coincident with the first publication of "Harmonious" is Brossard's contribution to *The Politics of Poetic Form*, "Poetic Politics," in which she argues that while a text "shows its politics in the writing" (78), it "becomes political"(80) when it is read. It becomes political because it makes "space for the unthought" (81) and can transform anger, ecstasy and desire into "social meaning" (81). However the reader needs to engage their training in perspective, theme, discourse and style to become a *non-conformist* reader and find "a space for new experience – travelling through meaning while simultaneously producing meaning" (79).

How does the writer invite the reader into articulation and the production of meaning? How does the text encourage a *non-conformist* reader? The suggestions scattered through "Harmonious" insistently take one back to the body. The writer is "troubled" by any movement that leaves desire behind (14): desire in most hegemonic discourse is constructed by the Lacanian symbolic as that thing in us that cannot be represented, therefore always already a loss or absence. But for the installed individual, desire is the prompt to recognise the not-yet-said. To leave behind desire is to hand oneself over to representation and reproduction. Desire is awakened by "les coquilles roses de sens" ["coral shells of meaning"] both tongue and clitoris, that through rapture graft matter onto the postures of voice – but this isn't readily definable matter, it's "matière secrète, matière plus ronde, matière comme tes soupirs et d'autres liquides encore" ["secret matter, matter more round, matter like your sighs and other liquids yet" (14, 15)]. Later, the body is pointed, punctuated, and retains in its passionate readings and subtle gestures an incredible synchrony of sense that reminds us that all is not said – despite the symmetries of thought. The indistinct/undefineable voice and touch of the body ("nos mains [...] caressent bien indistinctement de la voix et de la paume, le corps humain qui a des seins.") compasses both the universal and particular, constructing the world "to the measure of our hands" when they caress "a human body [that] has breasts" (18, 19).

On the one hand the writer perceives that life can silence, circumscribe, reduce, and she uses this knowledge to draw energy from the cycles of tears and the dust/push of birth to make sure that she works in dreams, at night, articulating into voice (20, 21). On the other, when her skin is "chargée de cyprine et d'é-cho" ["full of cyprin of echo" (22, 23)] she smiles the inseparability of the bodily and thoughtful in a deep breath. In this state stable objects (representations) make time reverse in her breast, they split thought, bound to enlighten death: she knows all is not said because her heart is wrung (22, 23) with the *inédit* of materiality. And at times when "la mémoire a peur de ses bonds et [...] les nerfs au milieu du désir sont comblés de réponses" ["memory is afraid of leaping and desire is full of answers"], when she is not "débor-dant dans l'air d'énergie" ["brimming with the breath of energy"] she can be seduced or tempted toward cer-tainty and sentiment even though she knows that all is not said because "la lumière [...] fracture l'ombre" ["the action of light breaking shadow"] revives her enery for re-thinking (24). The final stanza outlines the dilem-ma: "nommer est encore fonction de rêve et d'espoir" ["to name is still a function of dream and hope"] because women are still invisibly embodied in repre-sentation and need fictional form to participate fully in society. They need the fictional stability of installation that can insist on its position in discursive knowledge. Yet in the fictional, "entre la conversation urbaine et la tradition" ["between cultured conversation and tradi-tion"] it is vertiginously cold, we are left freezing at the edge of articulation that requires a precipitous projec-tion of oneself beyond fiction. Here it is the bodily presence of tears, in "la matière volatile des larmes" [their "volatile materiality"] that reminds us that despite the strange sweat of the *true* settling representations onto our *life*, all is not said (26, my translations).

To a significant extent the acknowledgement and recognition of the not-yet-said is at the centre of what an 'artist' does in the modern period of the Western world, a period Brossard's texts designate as *baroque*, the shift to humanist values in the seventeenth century. But the recognised writer-as-artist in the modern world has usually dealt with issues close to subject-hood, because they have come from the same socio-political grouping as those who hold and shape power. As such, their articulations have precisely addressed the repressions of representation, and could be perceived to transgress or oppose them because the representation/fiction/articulation border is so narrow. The precipice is not so high. Criticism has usually defined such attempt at articulation as "transcendent," because in habitual post-Cartesian fashion they hold language itself to be inadequate to the real: the limits of language have to be transcended by the artist in order to fiction-alise the real, to bring it into representation. Not that writers do this, and their increasing focus through the past three centuries on process and the not-yet-said, may be an indication of their frustration with the description. But this is how critics have expressed what they do: one could say that because he is a subject the modern artist is always gendered male.

From Transgression to Vision

Brossard attests to two specific changes in her life in 1974: motherhood and lesbian life (see *These Our Mothers*). They coincide with her decision to replace "transgression" with "marginality and vision." She refers to these two life changes as gaining "carnal knowledge," which led her to put aside "opposition" for "value" (*PP* 76). "Carnal knowledge" is the incontrovertible rooting of flesh and skin in "motive," that moves beyond the "object of desire" to vision (*PP* 74). These comments are followed by the claim that the "text" of language "calls for *vision* rather than subversion. It calls for awareness, concentration, sharpness. Vision goes beyond transgression because it brings forth new material" (82). Slightly earlier, in "Memory: Hologram of Desire" Brossard speaks of memory as the field/song [champs/chant] of vision: the memories and memory of women need to find fictional form because an "actualising memory" is "one that initiates presence in the world" (3). Women's memories, in "becoming visible and exposed in public... help[...] us to expand our field of vision (9). At the same time memory is the "hologram of desire," a "synchrony" of real life, imagination and "desire's fullness" (9). Yet the hologram does not retain the carnal knowledge of the lesbian body.

In "Writing as Trajectory" memory's part in vision is further clarified. The trajectory of writing toward vision is "the momentum of energy" (180) that combines the body and its "circulation of energy" with language and with writing: the body provides "for a network of associations out of which we create our mental environment [...] we imagine far beyond what we in fact see, hear or taste" (*PP* 73), and writing shapes that energy through language to suggest "solutions which can unknot social patterns of violence and death" (*PP* 74).[3] But writing "toward vision" is not a unitary action that leaves transgression completely behind. First, the individual's body has to "re-member childhood and to untie the knots that have formed in its throat (*WT* 180), a "ritual of trembling" that is a recognition of the unsaid in one's life, the process of memory. To enter the social world an individual needs to write in language that discursive or ideological power can recognise. If we choose to write for the representative world of ideology we transgress, we come up against the "antagonistic and hierarchical structure of misogynistic and patriarchal sense" that makes words invested with our energy "crash violently into the same word, the one invested with masculine experience," in what Brossard calls the "ritual with shock" (*WT* 181).

If instead we write for the discursive world we engage the "ritual with sliding" which subtly negotiates with power. All language connotes through semantic and metaphoric circuits that produce an "aura," "odour," or "tempo." "Ritual with sliding" displaces "slightly but sufficiently the semantic aura of words in such a way that they produce an unforeseeable resonance without alteration in the signifier" (182). The energy charge of this concentration on "sonority," "orthography," "usual sense," "potential polysemy" and "etymology" produces an effect that "conducts sense well beyond the signified," and "she who writes displaces imperceptibly but *radically* the order of the world" (182). "Ritual with sliding" fictionalises, reinvents language for the discursive, negotiates with hegemonic power, has direct social and political effect. At the same time it needs motivation, and I would argue, it finds this largely in the "ritual with breath" which multiplies "energy by modulating it to the rhythm most appropriate to thought in the body" (183). These four rituals are not separable, although they may be differently weighted. Together they make a "space for the existence of the woman subject and her desire [...] But [...] above all an unedited [articulation of the not-yet-said] space in which the unthought of the world suddenly takes the form of evidence" (184).

The Complications of the Body

Brossard describes the ritual of breath as an activity about "tonality," "music made of silence and harmony" that is "practised absolutely without mask" (*WT* 183). Most of her poetry engages us into some insight into the workings of the ritual of breath, and a different kind of engagement with it is offered by the text "Only a Body to Measure Reality By." Here the lesbian body, which has "felt the presence of the other woman as vital in your life [...] develops a skin so soft that it almost becomes a personal proof of faith in each woman" (9). The "radiant" lesbian body situates "on the side of *insoumission* [the not-compliant]." It begins as "our solitude, our only certitude," but because "the body has eyes to see, ears to listen, a memory to fantasize and words to compare, so it is, we are not alone anymore": we need "to read the in-between you and me" (5).

The extended sub-title of the piece, published from the Ravenscroft Lecture given with Daphne Marlatt in 1996, includes "Writing the In-Between." The harmonious lesbian body is not simply a body with many masks like difference, utopia and performance, but a body in touch with other bodies. This is the single element that makes it possible to turn away from transgression toward value, away from ideology to moral considerations. If the first step is to recognise the reductiveness of the representations of subjecthood, the second to separate the fictionality of installation from the fiction of the subject position and its shadow, the third is to delineate the body for articulation as one that will be able to control the slide back into installation. The isolated hologram cannot do this, but the necessary in-between negotiations of the harmonious les-

bian body can. What makes the concept philosophical-
ly different and challenging is that it does not suggest
an isolated alternative, despite the lingering signification of its *utopian* tendency. The "harmonious" body is
complicated because it is anti-transcendent and
focused on materiality, while simultaneously it creates
effects, articulations that can emerge into and change
the discursive, and may even become new representations or characters. The intellectual complexity is
focussed through Brossard's brief commentary on
beauty: as she notes in "Harmonious," if the materiality of the real were to fail/fall, it would strand us without warning, "la peau hésitante entre les philosophies
et l'aube" ["skin hesitating between philosophies and
dawn"] in "la vaste complication de la beauté" ["the
vast complication of beauty" (*TD* 16-17)].

Skin "hesitates" in the complication of beauty
because beauty occurs when articulations erupt into
the discursive. When the *inédit* is recognised by ideological or hegemonic systems, when it acquires fictional if not representative power, the not-yet-said is made
public, explodes with certainty into *fit* the first time,
and thereafter settles, "s'installe." Beauty marks the
point where social meaning is first given to articulations. In *Mauve Desert* "« La beauté est avant la réalité»,
d'une antériorité polysémique, impensable [...] La
beauté précède le désir, son fragment, l'histoire, la
coupe transversale de la réalité et de la fiction"
["'Beauty is before reality,' of a polysemic, unthinkable

antecedence [...] Beauty precedes desire, its fragment, history, the transection of reality and fiction"]. Beauty precedes reality because without representation reality cannot be recognised. It transects reality and fiction because it is both the source of representation and the presence of installation. The notes in *Mauve Desert* then go on to distinguish between the production of beauty that "prend forme dans le chaud du ventre de l'espèce [et] se transforme, langage, bris, miroitement, séduction: la beauté, angle de réflexion, neurone sélectif, langue à la source" ["takes shape in the warm belly of the species [and] transforms itself, language, break, shimmering, seduction: beauty, angle of reflection, selective neuron, source tongue"], and beauty as sustained eruption into *fit* that is the "Beauté froide de l'éternel, la beauté intimide" ["Cold beauty of the eternal, beauty intimidates"], "la beauté achève en nous l'intime, oui, menace suprêmement comme un langage froid" (160) ["beauty puts an end to intimacy in us, yes, threatens supremely like a cold language," makes an image into an astounding installation (145-6)].

The translator in *Baroque at Dawn* speaks of beauty as an enchantment, a "sentiment de pouvoir toucher à la lumière" (217) ["feeling that we can reach out and touch light" (213)]. But she also says that we need this conceptual sensation that the image *fits*. Indeed the Writer, having said that she doesn't write "any more" (205), is revived by the beauty of a fountain in Montréal, a response that allows her to "exist"

(234) just as she "existed" in Buenos Aires when writing her previous novel (212). Beauty is allied to *truth* in a profoundly Keatsian manner: it is eternal and cold, but at the same time like Keats' urnmaker, full of the complications of politics and the necessity to reinvent language and make recognisable the not-yet-said, and pregnant with evidence for value and moral action. Beauty is produced in the belly of the writer/text/reader.

The Body of the Inédit: Selfhood and Knowledge

Whatever verbal beauty becomes in the discursive or ideological, it comes from the hard labour on words we have undertaken during articulation, during the process of creating the not-yet-said, the *inédit*, the "objects of thought and emotion that can be shared" (*FA* 336). This work is also work on the self, but if the self is represented in the Lacanian symbolic, installed into the discursive, how is it present in the *inédit*? the harmonious lesbian body? The exploration of poetics and rhetoric made available by Brossard's critical writings is also a philosophical exploration of selfhood and of knowledge. For we cannot know that we exist if there is no other person to confirm our existence, just as we do not know that we know unless someone else shares the articulation as knowledge.

One text that braids beauty, selfhood and knowledge into close proximity is *La nuit verte du Parc*

Labyrinthe [Green Night in Labyrinth Park], which opens the "Premier Tournant" ["First Bend"] with the comment that life sets pronouns "tout autour du je dans le but de reconnaître, en nous, les autres sans trop de collision" ["all about the I in order to recognize, within us, the others, without too many collisions"], and concludes that while the sea "fait des fentes dans la vie des pronoms" ["creates fissures in the political life of pronouns"], destabilizing the I, so the pronouns are at times transformed into "d'essentielles figures" ["essential figures"]. Somewhere here is *life*, not as a principle that "s'épuise en anecdotes" ["wears itself out in anecdotes"] but life "dans la bouche qui énonce le principe. Salive, bactéries, langue, muqueuses, palais" (11) ["in the mouth that speaks the principle. Saliva, bacteria, tongue, mucus, palate" (27)]. And the political purpose of *Labyrinth* is to "seek the principle" in the bodily mouth of the speaker.

As a political text, it shares with the reader the activity of "making political" by understanding what is "in the mouth" of the writer. The writer first offers us the "story" or "labyrinth," into which she then walks, describing eleven bends: each of which excavates a strategy for understanding emotion and thought. If we take guidance from the final line of the opening labyrinth, the text outlines possible rhetorical manoeuvres, "I am breathing in rhetoric, in the never ending process of hope" (10, 26, 42). The "First Bend" displays the ambivalent rhetoric of *Politics* which "can be like a spell if you can't spell your name with a woman in mind" (11, 27). The "Second Bend" follows the history of the writer as someone who found the explanations of heterosexual discourse painful but who in time generated so many questions about alternative discourses that she learned to distance herself, flying so constantly among these archipelagos of discourse that she had diverted the initial set of explanations into other routes.

With the "Third Bend" the writer reads one phrase from the labyrinth "le châle bleu qui glissait sur les épaules de Simone" (13) ["the blue shawl slipping from Simone's shoulders"] as an image that persists as a "relais de ferveur" ["fervent relay" (29)], insisting on engagement without resolution. The "Fourth Bend" is a commentary on the word "pays"/ "country" as a contradiction between a unifying lesbian language and its destruction of "lesbian lives," speaking again to the difficulty of distinguishing between the discursive or installed self, and that of the material, the self as bodily enigma. The difficulty is underwritten in the "Fifth Bend" which returns to "image," of "quand la neige s'installe sur ton front" (15) "[when snowflakes fall on your forehead" (31)]. an image of the impartiality of Death that hints at the enigma of material existence. It knows its enigmatic self only in engagement with other human beings. This does not mean that it is the same as other human beings, but that it needs contact with them to know itself. In 'Body' Brossard says that the body can "slip from I to we, from us to them when we talk of freedom and the future," but also that the body cares about its "singularity and intimacy" (6). Later, in "Elsewhere," the title rephrases this: "I like to say we and look elsewhere" (60).

The necessity for another person is examined in the "Sixth Bend," which presents *"je thème* [...] le *je t'aime* lesbien" ["*I theme* [...] the lesbian *I love you*"] as forming a skin of language that encompasses writer, reader and text in a single body, but also the speaking, the sounds that pleasure makes "quand il longe un énoncé" (16) ["as it rubs up against a speaking" (32)], to find the difference among people pleasurable. The "Seventh Bend" offers lesbian speaking as "Épaules qui longent la nuit comme un absolu *in the never ending process of hope*" ["Shoulders that rub up against the night like an absolute *in the never ending process of hope*"]. "Breathing in rhetoric" becomes the lesbian speaking. *"Breathe your silence, respira en tu memoria,* impregnate rhetoric" becomes the strategy of articulating the lesbian body as she feels "ma langue glisser sur la chair très tendre du mot clitoris" ["my tongue slipping on the very tender flesh of the word clitoris"], and simultaneously "Je taille [...] la subjectivité de celle qui me ressemble avec sa bouche" (17) ["shaping the subjectivity of she whose mouth resembles mine" (33)]. The shared skin of articulation effects and affects the installation and the subject.

The "Eighth Bend" curiously slips into untranslated French, seemingly purposively because the Spanish translation also retains the French, as it unfurls the phrase "des signifiants mystérieux au coin des lèvres" (18) ["mysterious signifiers in the curve of lips" (34)]. And reading becomes translation. Such a process of translation and the text the reader creates for herself suggest that one way of thinking about the process of articulation, the way images drift into ideas without our conscious or subjected awareness, the way values emerge in the stretching of words into touch of the other person, the way the apprehension of the enigma of self materialises, is to place them in the present, in the moment, saying it must be simultaneous, like rhetoric which provides us with the tools to act in 'probably-the-best' way in many situations, like rhetoric which does not pursue the truth (although it can describe it) but moral action. Work on immediate material rhetoric allows the writer-reader to "existe[r] dans la langue écrite parce que c'est là que je décide des pensées qui règlent les questions et les réponses que je donne à la réalité" (19) ["exist in written language because it is there that I decide the thoughts that settle the questions and answers I give to reality" (35)].

If most language is in myths and tears, representations and need from the not-yet-said, as the "Tenth Bend" suggests, the "Eleventh Bend" returns to lesbian space and a different kind of political rhetoric to that in the First. Here is a place on the archipelago that is not territory nor country, but in "des signifiants mystérieux aux coins des lèvres" ["the mysterious signifiers in the curve of her lips"], a "présence d'esprit" ["presence of spirit"]. This reading of the labyrinth has been an exploration of articulation at the same time as it is itself an articulation of that space, a space delineated for the writer in writing and words. An exploration full of danger, for in loosening the discourse of reality one may lose oneself, and so in preparation/ as a precaution she first loved "longuement une femme qui comme moi s'était plongée dans beaucoup de livres, sans jamais avoir peur de se tremper dans le rêve et la réalité" (21) ["long and well a woman who, like myself, had dived into many books, without ever being afraid of drenching herself in dream and reality" (37)]. As Brossard notes in "Poetic Politics," "Sooner or later the body of writing pays for its untamed desire of beauty and knowledge" (81).

The Body and Virtual Reality

The arc of thinking from *Installations* to *Labyrinth* builds complex but load-bearing architecture – which makes *Baroque at Dawn* and some subsequent remarks unusual. *Baroque at Dawn* problematises the concept of articulation in the moment, with its focus on presence,[4] by writing about a technology, virtual reality, that seems to mimic what articulation does. The photographer Irène Mage has recently turned away from camera photography to the speed and surface of computer-

generated images, and she comments to the novelist
Cybil Noland that as a writer she is still a naive thinker,
working on "des passions et des motivations. Votre art
[...] reste profondément moral" (87) ["passions and
motivations. Your art [...] remains profoundly moral"
(79)]. In itself this is not unusual, but in its reappear-
ance in subsequent essays as a source of concern and
anxiety,[5] Brossard alerts her readers/listeners to the
strange manner in which the *body* is being eviscerated
by technology. As she warns in the "Avant-Propos" to a
recent collection of feminist essays in *Globe*, "voilà,
qu'après avoir décrété que nous refusions d'être des
femmes-objets, force est de constater que les biotechnologies du patriarcat *soft* sont en train de transformer
le corps en monnaie courante" (14) ["after having
decreed that women should refuse to be objects, it must
now be acknowledged that the biotechnologies of *soft*
patriarchy are in the process of transforming the body
into its exchange value"]. And she concludes,
"Qu'allons-nous devoir inventer pour que l'amour de
la vie et l'espoir de changement ne nous transforment
pas en Vénus digitales ou en dociles consommatrices
de *réalité*?" (15) ["What are we going to have to invent
so that love of life and hope for change don't transform
us into digital Venuses or docile consumers of *reality*?"
(trans. LHF)]. The second alternaive of that last query
is at the heart of Brossard's writing, the first, the
"Vénus digitales," is new.

Baroque at Dawn posits the virtual reality of computer technology as a possible analogue for the fiction created by writing. It constructs a present that puts Cybil Noland, the author of the novel being written about, into 'double time', where writing becomes "une volonté de surface où le sens ne risquait pas de faire mal" (176) ["a desire to surf on words, eliminating risk of harm by meaning" (172)]. Later she is "possédée par une envie irrésistible de détails" ["overcome by an irresistible desire for details"] and "Les états d'âme, de rêve, de lucidité et de laisser râler se succédaient" (180-1) ["states of mind, of dream, lucidity and laissez-belly-ache followed" (177)] that have her alternating reality and fiction 'hurtling on' at speed. That night she dreams of the woman in Hyde Park who is quoting from *Alice in Wonderland* the same words that open "Only One Body for Comparison: Writing the In-Between." It is as if the enigma of self has disappeared, the absence of any other person has left Cybil Noland floating in a fiction that is impossible to distinguish from representation or materiality: fiction as virtual reality. The eyes are vulnerable to the new visual technologies, for the eye appears instantaneous, as opposed to rhetoric and the word which need time. The difference is time. Its availability. Silence, its marker.

In *Baroque at Dawn* the writer of the novel about Cybil Noland writing a novel cannot continue to write after that radical deformation of presence until, through translation, presence begins to make material sense once more. With someone else, here the translator in person, the material present can happen. The apparent immediacy of virtual reality erases the differences between the symbolic, the fictional and the material. But, like any technology, any human craft, it has its own rhetoric. The problem lies in the speed of its change and the effective impact it has on society before we can grasp and engage with that rhetoric, the knowledge it instantiates, the moral action it enables. Despite arguing that "Poetry is simultaneous, in the moment, present: prose dilutes tension, projects into temporal dimension, slows desire" (*FA* 319), Brossard also knows that all writing presupposes "deferral and delay and difference" (Aut*her* 2). Much earlier, in *Journal Intime,* she says that writing slows down between each word, that she had to learn to see the whites coming "The white that one calls white spaces are in fact so filled with thoughts, with words, with sensations, with hesitations and with chances to be taken" (*FA* 342). And much later, she notes the importance of silence as material presence for writing, for silence, which takes place in slow time, "can activate the white on the page, the light that makes it tremble around intimacy" ("The Most Precious Things" 5). This last essay, given as a paper at the University of Calgary, is again subtitled to connect to the other human body: "The most precious things in the future will be water and silence And a human voice."

I would argue that for many first time readers, reading *Baroque at Dawn* is like reading a text through which the images pass too swiftly, through which syntax hurtles our body. It provokes a virtual reality of intense presence and vertiginous nausea, a necessarily relativist knowledge that may not even be knowing because we can only know that we know if another person offers context, and the self-focussed action that results can hardly be moral. This is partly because technically the writing is *prose*, and most western readers are schooled to consume *prose* swiftly, possibly so well-schooled in novelistic technique (from both book and film) that they are experts at this kind of reading and take too much for granted. Yet any carefully trained reader knows that reading, like writing, needs time. Re-reading, supportively, comparatively, even with other readers as I do in the classroom, and making differences, the text invites us into articulation. It sensitises me to points of touch that release energy into the material through work on the *inédit*, it integrates another language into my skin. The knowledge I recognise is shared, I learn to value the differences I have made in comparison, and any action I take is located in the detail of shared lives.

The final section of *Baroque at Dawn* "One Single Body for Comparison," echoes a warning from "Le futur *dark*" ["The *Dark* Future"] that in art "la tentation est toujours grande de comparer à la réalité [...] de réassigner dans le réel la portée énigmatique de l'oeuvre" (165) ["it's always very tempting to draw a comparison with reality [...] to reassign the enigmatic import of the work in our own conception of reality" (161)]. We have to train ourselves to use our "seul corps" ["single body"] to find "les mots nécessaires" ["the necessary words"] to "compare," to hold a "corps de mémoire pour inventer et progresser vers le silence" (219) ["body of memory for inventing and progressing toward silence" (215)]. Part of this training, as the criticism explores and the book displays, is training in the rhetoric of poetic: in stress, rhythm, syntax, sound, image, topic, theme. Part of the training is understanding the energy of the body: for example its skeleton, its *elasticity*, the effect of the vowels (231, 227) – those emotive sounds resounding without the muscular check of consonants through the body. And part of this training is learning to work the body with others. Here in *Baroque at Dawn*, the writer and translator are both looking for the "ailleurs du *par ailleurs*" ["other hand part of *on the other hand*"] not wanting to compromise "le sens du récit, la configuration des destins" (230) ["the meaning of the story, the configuration of destinies" (226)]. So that in conclusion the writer writes "Un seul corps pour composer avec la jeune lumière du jour et la lueur des mots dans les yeux de la traductrice" ["One single body to compound with the young light of day and the words shining in the translator's eyes"], asking "Qu'allons-nous chercher dans le silence d'autrui, les yeux alléchés par la proximité et les comparaisons qui font tourbillon de vaste moi? Qu'allons-nous chercher là dans le réflexe du rapprochement?"

(260) ["What are we to look for in the silence of others, with eyes enticed by proximity and whirligig comparisons day vastating us? What are we to look for in the very desire for comparisons and closeness?" (256)].

The body we measure reality by is a treasured enigma of self, but it is compounded and comparative when encompassed by the skin of language. Brossard's own definition of energy is as a term she uses "to analyze those forces in the process of literary creation." "Imagination goes through the skin the skin is energy" (*FA* 338), and as the vast permeable lung of articulation it breathes the material reality of the *inédit* into sound and resonance, into words, into installation, into fiction and yes, into representation. It makes it possible for the powerful to hear those erased from or marginal to power. Sprung by desire it is motivated by the material reality of the located body, a location created by the self and others working on the detail of lived lives: making differences through knowing and in the making learning to value, so that we may make moral actions.

This is how I feel when I read the novels with other people to compare. And this is how I feel now, having had the opportunity to write in detail through the vertiginous fear of the critical rhetoric. On reflection I would say that it was the process of engaging with both the texts and their translations that opened a way to breathe through the skin of language, find a bodily presence in the words, and make new material. Rather like the writer in *Baroque at Dawn*.

Notes

1. Many of Brossard's texts are interwoven. Hence, for example, 'Memory' is infused into 'Trajectory.' It has not been possible to indicate all double sources in this essay.

2. For bilingual editions cited in this essay page references are given simultaneously to French and English texts.

3. See also work on *corps/texte/writing* in Marlatt's "Mauve"/*Salvage*. Red Deer: Red Deer College Press 1991. 98.

4. See *She would be* 109, 115, 129, but also concern with an isolated "I" 91.

5. See also "Fluid Arguments" 332 and "Au*ther*" 2.

Works Cited

Brossard, Nicole. "Au*ther*." 1997. From typescript provided by S. Rudy.

——. "La matière harmonieuse manoeuvre encore/ Harmonious Matter Still Manoeuvres." Trans. Caroline Bergvall. *Typhon dru*. London and Saxmundham, Suffolk: Reality Street Editions, 1997. 7-27.

——. "The most precious things in the future will be water and silence and a human voice." 1999/ 2001. Presentation to Graduate Student conference, University of Western Ontario, and English Department, University of Alberta. From typescript provided by S. Rudy.

Butler, Judith. *Bodies that Matter: on the discursive limits of 'sex'*. London: Routledge. 1993.

Hunter, Lynette. *Critiques of Knowing: Situated Textualities in Science, Computing and the Arts*. London: Routledge, 1999.

Works by Nicole Brossard

(Acronyms used in essays are shown in brackets, references are not given for the many books, journals and other periodicals in which pieces by Brossard have been anthologized; many shorter pieces are not included here: of particular importance are those that appeared regularly for many years in *La Barre du Jour* and *La Nouvelle Barre du Jour*, including the particularly important tradition of special issues on women and women's writing inaugurated by Brossard in 1975.)

Poetry

"Aube à la saison." *Trois*. Cahier 12. Montréal: Les Presses de l'A.G.É.U.M., 1965. 37-68. (AS)

Mordre en sa chair. Montréal: Estérel, 1966. (*MC*)

L'écho bouge beau. Montréal: Estérel-Quoi, 1968. (*EB*)

Le centre blanc. Montréal: Orphée, 1970. (*CB*)

Suite logique. Montréal: L'Hexagone, 1970. (*SL*)

Mécanique jongleuse. Paris: Génération, 1973.

Mécanique jongleuse, suivi de *Masculin Grammaticale*. Montréal: L'Hexagone, 1974. (*MJ*)

La partie pour le tout. Montréal: L'Aurore, 1975. (*P*)

Le centre blanc. Poèmes 1965-1975. Montréal: L'Hexagone, 1978.

D'arcs de cycle la dérive. Gravure de Francine Simonin. Saint-Jacques-le-Mineur: Édition de la Maison, 1979.

Amantes. Montréal: Éditions Quinze, 1980. (*AM*) Audio-cassette recording of *Amantes* by Nicole Brossard. Artlect. 1989. 2ᵉ éd. *Amantes*, suivi de *Le sens apparent* et de *Sous la langue*. Montréal: L'Hexagone, 1998: 7-117.

Daydream Mechanics. Trans. Larry Shouldice. Toronto: Coach House Press, 1980. Trans. of *MJ*.

Double impression. Poèmes et textes 1967-1984. Montréal: L'Hexagone, 1984. (*DI*)

Domaine d'écriture. Montréal: *La Nouvelle Barre du jour* 154, 1985.

L'aviva. Montréal: La Nouvelle Barre du Jour, 1985.

Brossard and Daphne Marlatt. *Mauve*. Montréal: La Nouvelle Barre du Jour, 1985.

Brossard and Daphne Marlatt. *Character/ Jeu de lettres*. Montréal: La Nouvelle Barre du jour, 1986.

Lovhers. Trans. Barbara Godard. Toronto: Guernica, 1986. Trans. of AM (*L*)

Sous la langue/ Under Tongue. Trans. Susanne de Lotbinière-Harwood. Montréal:

L'Essentielle, éditrices; Charlottetown: Gynergy Books, 1987. 2ᵉ éd. *Amantes*, suivi de *Le sens apparent* et de *Sous la langue*. Montréal: L'Hexagone, 1998: 191-197.

Installations (avec et sans pronoms). Trois-Rivières: Les Écrits des Forges; Pantin: Le Castor Astral, 1989. (*If*)

A tout regard. Montréal: Les Éditions de la Nouvelle Barre du Jour, 1989.

"La matière harmonieuse manoeuvre encore." *The Massachussette Review*, 31. 1-2 (Spring-Summer 1990). Trans. Lise Weil.

Typhon dru. Paris: Collectif Génération, 1990.

La subjectivité des lionnes. Bruxelles: Le Buisson ardent/ L'Arbre à paroles, 1991.

Langues obscures. Montréal: L'Hexagone, 1992.

La nuit verte du parc Labyrinthe/ Green Night of Labyrinth Park/ La noche verde del parque Laberinto. Trans. Lou Nelson and Marina Fe. Laval: Éditions Trois, 1992. (*NV/ GN*)

Flesh, song(e) et promenade. Montréal: Lèvres urbaines 23, 1993.

Typhon dru, suivi de *La matière harmonieuse manoeuvre encore*. Trans. Caroline Bergvall. London: Reality Street Editions, 1997. Trans. of *TD*.

Vertige De L'Avant-Scène. Trois-Rivières: Écrits des Forges/ L'Orange bleue Éditeur, 1997. (*VA*)

Instalationes. Trans. Monica Mansour. Mexico: Unam/ Aldus; Trois-Rivières: Écrits des Forges, 1997. Trans. of *Installations*.

Au présent des veines. Trois-Rivières: Écrits des Forges; Herborn, Luxembourg: Phi; La Réunion: Grand Océan, 1999. (*AV*)

Musée de l'os et de l'eau. Engravings by Catherine Farish. Saint-Hippolyte: Éditions du Noroît; Saussines, France: Cadex Éditions, 1999.

Vertigo del proscenio. Trans. Monica Mansour. Mexico: Le Toucan de Virginie, 2000. Trans. of *VA*.

Installations (with and without pronouns). Trans. Erin Mouré and Robert Majzels. Winnipeg: Gordon Shillingford Publishing/ The Muses Company, 2000. Trans. of *I*. (*Ie*)

En el presente de la pulsacion. Trans. Sara Cohen and Alicia Genovese. Buenos Aires: Botella al Mar, 2000. Trans. of *AV*.

"A Blind Chameleon Always Takes the Proper Colour for Camouflage," "sans titre." *Verdure*. 5- 6 (2002): 38-43.

Namestititve. Trans. Brane Mozetic. Ljubljana: Zalozba Skuc, 2002. Trans. of *I*.

Cahier de roses & de civilisation. Engravings by Francine Simonin. *Écritures 2*. Trois-Rivières: Éditions d'Art Le Sabord, 2003. (*CR*)

Museum of Bone and Water. Trans. Erin Mouré and Robert Majzels. Toronto: Anansi, 2003. Trans. of *Musée de l'os et de l'eau*.

Shadow Soft et soif. Trans. Guy Bennett. Los Angeles: Seeing Eye Books. 2003. Translation of unpublished poems.

Fiction

Un livre. Montréal: Éditions du Jour, 1970. 2e éd. Montréal: Éditions Quinze, 1980. (*UL*)

Sold-out. Étreinte/illustration. Montréal: Éditions du Jour, 1973. 2e éd. Éditions Quinze, 1980. (*SO*)

French kiss. Étreinte-exploration. Montréal: Éditions du Jour, 1974. 2e éd. Éditions Quinze, 1980. (*FKf*)

A Book. Trans. Larry Shouldice. Toronto: Coach House Press, 1976. Trans. of *UL*. 2e éd. *The Blue Books*. Toronto: Coach House Books, 2003: 15-115. (*AB*)

Turn of a Pang. Trans. Patricia Claxton. Toronto: Coach House Press, 1976. Trans. of *SO*. 2e éd. *The Blue Books*. Toronto: Coach House Books, 2003: 117-225. (*TP*)

L'amèr ou le chapitre effrité (fiction théorique). Montréal: Éditions Quinze, 1977. 2e éd. Montréal: L'Hexagone, 1988. (*A*)

Le sens apparent. Paris: Flammarion, 1980. 2e éd. *Amantes*, suivi de *Le sens apparent* et de *Sous la langue*. Montréal: L'Hexagone, 1998: 119-190. (*SA*)

Picture Theory. Montréal: Éditions Nouvelle Optique, 1982. 2e éd. Montréal: L'Hexagone, 1989. (*PTf*)

These Our Mothers. Or: The Disintegrating Chapter. Trans. Barbara Godard. Toronto: Coach House Press, 1983. Trans. of *A*. (*TM*)

French Kiss. Or: A Pang's Progress. Trans. Patricia Claxton. Toronto: Coach House Press, 1986. Trans. of FKf. 2e éd. *The Blue Books*. Toronto: Coach House Books, 2003: 227-341. (*FKe*)

Le désert mauve. Montréal: L'Hexagone, 1987. (*DM*)

Surfaces of Sense. Trans. Fiona Strachan. Toronto: Coach House Press, 1989. Trans. of *SA*. (*SS*)

Die Malvenfarbene. Trans. Traude Buhrmann. Berlin: Frauenoffensive, 1989. Trans. of *DM*.

Mauve Desert. Trans. Susanne de Lotbinière-Harwood. Toronto: Coach House Press, 1990. Trans. of *DM*. (*MD*)

Picture Theory. Trans. Barbara Godard. New York: Roof Books, 1990; Toronto: Guernica, 1991. Trans. of *PTf*. (*PTe*)

Baroque d'aube. Montréal: L'Hexagone, 1995. (*BA*)

El desierto malva. Trans. Monica Mansour. Mexico: Editorial Joaquin Mortiz, 1996. Trans. of *DM*.

Baroque at Dawn. Trans. Patricia Claxton. Toronto: McClelland & Stewart, 1997. Trans. of *BA*. (*BD*)

Barroco al alba. Trans. Pilar Giralt Gorina. Barcelone: Seix Barral, 1998. Trans. of *BA*.

Hier. Montréal: Québec/ Amérique, 2001. (*H*)

Selected Works of Prose, Theory, and Other Non-Fiction

"Blow up l'efficace." *La Barre du Jour*. 2.4 (1967): 11-15.

"D'une surface." *La Barre du Jour*. 25 (1970): 16-27.

"Énunciation (sic) Déformation ludique." *Stratégie*. 3-4 (1973)

"Vaseline." *La Barre du Jour*. 42 (1973): 11-17.

"Le cortex exubérant." *La Barre du Jour*. 44 (1974): 2-22.

"*E* muet mutant." *La Barre du Jour*. 50 (1975): 6-27. Trad. M.L. Taylor. *Ellipse*. 23-24 (1979): 44-63. (EM)

"La femme et l'écriture." *Liberté*. 18. 4-5 (1976): 10-13 *et passim*.

Brossard and France Théoret. "Préface." *La nef des sorcières*. Ed. Nicole Brossard; France Théoret. Montréal: Éditions Quinze, 1976. 7-13.

"L'écrivain." *La nef des sorcières*. Ed. Nicole Brossard; France Théoret. Montréal: Éditions Quinze, 1976. 73-80. 2e éd. Montréal: L'Hexagone, 1992. (E)

"La tête qu'elle fait." *La Barre du Jour*. 56-57 (1977): 83-92.

"L'avenir de la littérature québécoise." *Études françaises*. 13. 3-4 (1978): 383-93.

"Poésie engagée." *Revue de l'Université Laurentienne*. X.2 (1978): 121-25.

"Le sens apparent." *La Nouvelle Barre du Jour*. 75. (1979): 11-23.

"Les surfaces (Histoire d'écrire)." *La Nouvelle Barre du Jour*. 81 (1979): 69-80.

"The Writer." *A Clash of Symbols*. Trans. Linda Gaboriau. Toronto: The Coach House Press, 1979. 34-38. Trans. of (E).

Les têtes de pioche (1976-79). *Collection complète*. Montréal: Éditions du Remue-Ménage, 1980. (articles throughout by Brossard)

"Les stratégies du réel," "Simulation." *Les stratégies du réel/ The Story So Far 6*. Montréal: La Nouvelle Barre du Jour; Toronto: Coach House Press, 1979. 8-9, 147-171.

"Les traces du manifeste." *Tessera*. 6 (1989): VIII-XI.

"L'épreuve de la modernité." *La Nouvelle Barre du Jour*. 90-1 (1980): 55-68.

"Hilton." *La Nouvelle Barre du Jour*. 102 (1981): 77-86.

"Djuna Barnes: de profil moderne." *Mon héroïne*. Ed. Pol Pelletier. Montréal: Éditions du Remue-Ménage, 1981. 189-214.

"L'identité comme science-fiction de soi." *Identités collectives et changements sociaux*, Tome II. Toulouse: Privat, 1981. 391-95.

"Notes et fragments d'urgence." *Femmes et politique*. Ed. Yolande Cohen. Montréal: Le Jour Éditeur, 1981. 15-19.

Journal intime, ou Voilà donc un manuscrit. Montréal: Les Herbes Rouges, 1984. 2e éd. *Journal intime, ou Voilà donc un manuscrit*, suivi de *Oeuvre de chair et métonymies*. Montréal: Les Herbes rouges, 1998. (*JI*)

"La page du livre." *Women & Words. The Anthology/ Les Femmes et les mots. Une Anthologie* Ed. West Coast Editorial Collective. Madeira Park: Harbour Publishing Company, 1984. 126-29.

La lettre aérienne. Montréal: Éditions du Remue-Ménage, 1985. (*LA*)

"Access to Writing: Language Ritual." *Trivia (A Journal of Ideas)*. (1986).

"De radical à intégrales." *L'émergence d'une culture au féminin*. Ed. Marisa Zavalloni. Montréal: Éditions Saint-Martin, 1987. 163-74.

"Mouvements et stratégies de l'écriture de fiction." *Gynocritics. Feminist Approaches to Writing by Canadian and Québécoises Women/ La gynocritique. Approches féministes à l'écriture des canadiennes et québécoises*. Ed. Barbara Godard. Toronto: ECW Press, 1987. 227-30.

"Kind Skin My Mind." *Trivia (A Journal of Ideas)*. 12 (1988): 43-44.

"L'angle tramé du désir, éperdument." *La théorie, un dimanche*. Eds. Louky Bersianik, Nicole Brossard, Louise Cotnoir, Louise Dupré, Gail Scott, and France Théoret. Montréal: Éditions du Remue-Ménage, 1988. 11-33.

"Mémoire: Hologramme du désir." *La parole métèque*. 7 (1988): 6-8. (*MH*) Rpt. *Quebec Studies* 31 (Spring/Summer 2001): 8-11.

"Memory: Hologram of Desire." *Trivia (A Journal of Ideas)*. 13 (1988): 42-47.

The Aerial Letter. Trans. Marlene Wildeman. Toronto: The Women's Press, 1988. Trans. of *LA*. (*AL*)

La lettera aerea. Trans. Luisa Muraro. Florence: Editions Estro, 1990. Trans of *LA*.

"La version des femmes du réel." *La poésie de l'Hexagone*. Ed. Cécile Cloutier and Ben Shek. Montréal: L'Hexagone, 1990. 73-77.

"Le tueur n'était pas un jeune homme." *Polytechnique, 6 déc*. Eds. Louise Malette and Marie Chalouh. Montréal: Éditions du Remue-Ménage, 1990. 29-30.

"Poetic Politics." *The Politics of Poetic Form. Poetry and Public Policy*. Ed. Charles Bernstein. New York: Roof Books, 1990. 73-86. (*PP*)

"Autobiographie." *Contemporary Authors*, Autobiography Series.16. Eds. Joyce Nakamura; Susanne de Lotbinière-Harwood. Detroit, London: Gale Research Inc., 1992. 39-57.

Nicole Brossard and Michèle Causse. "Correspondance." *Trivia (A Journal of Ideas)*. (1992).

"Femme à la bouche ouverte pendant un bombardement." *Arcade* 1992: 7.

"Writing As a Trajectory of Desire and Consciousness." *Feminist Critical Negotiations*. Trans. Alice A. Parker. *Critical Theory. Interdisciplinary Approaches to Language, Discourse and Ideology*. 9. Ed. Alice A. Parker and Elizabeth A. Meese. Amsterdam, Philadelphia: John Benjamins Publishing Company, 1992. 179-85. (*WT*)

"Procession d'un oui qui va son énergie." *Mises en scène d'écrivains*. Ed. Mireille Calle. Sainte- Foy: Le Griffon d'argile; Grenoble: Presses universitaires de Grenoble, 1993. 63-71.

"Ludique critique et moderne. rebelle/ scribble." *Les discours féminins dans la littérature postmoderne au Québec*. Eds. Raija Koski, Kathleen Kells, and Louise Forsyth. San Francisco: EM Text, 1993: 107-111.

"Écrire la société: d'une dérive à la limite du réel et du fictif." *Philosophiques*. XXI.2 (1994): 303-20.

"Certain Words." *Collaboration in the Feminine. Writings on Women and Culture from Tessera*. Trans. Barbara Godard. Toronto: Second Story Press. 1994. 47-52.

Brossard and Louky Bersianik, Louise Cotnoir, Louise Dupré, Gail Scott. "What We Talk about on Sundays." *Collaboration in the Feminine. Writings on Women and Culture from Tessera*. Trans. Barbara Godard. Toronto: Second Story Press. 1994. 127-135.

"Le corps du personnage." *Tessera*, 19 (1995): 63-71.

Brossard and Daphne Marlatt. "Only a Body to Measure Reality By: Writing the In-Between." *Journal of Commonwealth Literature* 31.2 (1996): 5-17. (*OB*)

"Fluid Arguments." *Onward: Contemporary Poetry and Poetics*. Ed. P. Baker. New York: Peter Lang, 1996. 315-46. (*FA*)

"Oeuvre de chair et métonymies." *Femmes, corps et âme*. Montréal: Musée de la civilisation; XYZ Éditeur, 1996. 39-52. 2e éd. *Journal intime*, suivi de *Oeuvre de chair et métonymies*. Montréal: Les Herbes Rouges, 1998.

"Écriture lesbienne: stratégie de marque." *Les études gay et lesbiennes*. Ed. Didier Eribon. Paris: Centre George Pompidou, 1998. 51-56.

Elle serait la première phrase de mon prochain roman/ She Would Be the First Sentence of My Next Novel. Trans. Susanne de Lotbinière-Harwood. Toronto: Mercury Press, 1998. (*ES*)

"I like to say we and look elsewhere." Trans P. Joris. *Boundary 2: An International Journal of Literature and Culture*. 26.1 (1999): 60-2. Ed. C. Bernstein. '99 Poets/1999: An International Poetics Symposium.

"Vingt Pages entrecoupées de silence." *Les Écrits*. 95 (1999): 117-40.

"A State of Mind in the Garden." *Journal of Lesbian Studies* (2000): 35-40.

"Avant-propos." *Globe. Revue internationale d'études québécoises*. Theme: "Le vingtième siècle québécois des femmes." 3.2 (2000): 11-15. (*AP*)

"Écrivaine." *Le dernier livre du siècle. Deux américains enquêtent sur l'intelligentsia française au tournant du siècle*. Paris: Romillat, 2001. 252-256.

Nikki. Trans. Mitoko Hirabayashi and Bev Curran. Tokyo: Kokubunsha, 2000. Trans. of *JI*.

"Silence." *Le Devoir* (29 July 2002): A1,A8.

"Silence and a Human Voice: Vital Materials for a Future (excerpts)." *Verdure*. 5-6 (2002): 32- 37.

"Journal intime (extrait)," "An Intimate Journal (excerpt)." *Verdure*. Trans. Barbara Godard. *Verdure*. 5-6 (2002): 72-90 (from publication of *An Intimate Journal* by Mercury Press).

Intimate Journal or Here's a Manuscript, followed by *Words of Flesh and Metonymies*. Trans. Barbara Godard. Toronto: The Mercury Press, 2004. Trans. of (JI) and *Oeuvre de chair et métonymies*.

Écrire l'horizon du fragment. Paroisse Notre-Dame-des-Neiges, Québec: Éditions Trois-Pistoles, 2004.

Theatre

"Narrateur et personnages" (dramatique d'une demi-heure). Radio-Canada. 1971. (unpublished)

"L'écrivain." *La nef des sorcières*. Ed. Nicole Brossard and France Théoret. Montréal: Éditions Quinze, 1976. 73-80. 2e éd. Montréal: L'Hexagone, 1992. (*E*)

"Une impression de fiction dans le rétroviseur." Radio-Canada. 1978. (unpublished)

"The Writer." Trans. Linda Gaboriau. *A Clash of Symbols*. Toronto: Coach House Press, 1979. *Fireweed*. 5-6 (1979-80): 106-117. Trans. of (E)

"La falaise." Radio-Canada. 1985. (unpublished)

Anthologies

Les stratégies du réel/ The Story So Far 6. Montréal: Coach House Press; Toronto: La Nouvelle Barre du Jour, 1979. (*SR*)

Brossard and Lisette Girouard. *Anthologie de la poésie des femmes au Québec (1677-1988).* Montréal: Éditions du Remue-Ménage, 1991. 2ᶜ éd. *Anthologie de la poésie des femmes au Québec des origines à nos jours.* Montréal: Éditions du Remue-Ménage, 2003.

Poèmes à dire la francophonie, 38 poètes contemporains. Paris: Castor Astral/ CNDP, 2002.

Cinema

Brossard and Luce Guilbeault. *Some American Feminists: New York 1976.* Montréal: Office national du film, 1976. (Interviews with Kate Millett, Betty Friedan, Ti-Grace Atkinson, Rita May Brown, and Simone de Beauvoir)

Selected Interviews and Studies
of the Works of Nicole Brossard

Andersen, Marguerite. "Women of Skin and Thought." *The Women's Review of Books*. IV.4 (January 1987): 16.

Bayard, Caroline. "Subversion is the Order of the Day." *Essays in Canadian Writing* 1977: 17- 25.

——. "Entrevue avec Nicole Brossard." *Avant-postes*. Toronto: Presses Porcépic, 1978.

——. *The New Poetics in Canada and Quebec*. Toronto: University of Toronto Press, 1989.

Bayard, Caroline and Jack David. "Entrevue." *Les Lettres québécoises*. 4 (1976): 34-37.

Beaudet, André. "Le Récit rouge." *Brèche*. 2 (1973): 59-70.

——. "Gynécophonie-s," suivi de "Dessins, oblique, profils." *La Nouvelle Barre du Jour*. 88 (1980): 113-30.

Beausoleil, Claude. *Le motif de l'identité dans la poésie québécoise 1830-1995*. Montréal: Estuaire, 1996.

——. "Le Sens apparent/ Amantes." *Livres et auteurs québécois 1980*. Québec: Les Presses de l'Université Laval, 1981. 95-98.

Bonenfant, Joseph. "Nicole Brossard, hauteur d'un texte." *Voix et images du pays*. IX (1975): 63-85.

Campeau, Francine. "Nicole Brossard sur la scène utopique." *La Parole métèque*. 5 (1988): 32- 33.

Conley, Katharine. "The Spiral as Moebius Strip: Inside/ Outside *Le Désert mauve*." *Quebec Studies*. 18 (1994): 149-58.

——. "Going for Baroque in the Twentieth Century: From Desnos to Brossard." *Québec Studies*. 31 (2001): 12-23.

Cooke, Nathalie. "Entrevue avec Nicole Brossard." *Arc*. 32 (1994): 55-61.

Cotnoir, Louise, Lise Guevremont, Claude Beausoleil, and Hugues Corriveau. "Interview with Nicole Brossard on *Picture Theory*." *Canadian Fiction Magazine*. 47 (1983): 122-35.

Couillard, Marie and Francine Dumouchel. "Symphonie Féministe." *Gynocritics/ La gynocritique. Feminist Approaches to Writing by Canadian and Québécoises Women/ Approches féministes à l'écriture des Canadiennes et Québécoises*. Ed. Barbara Godard. Toronto: ECW Press, 1987. 77-83.

Curran, Beverley. "'Je suis une Geisha devant mon ordinateur': Nicole Brossard in Japanese Translation." *Verdure*. 5-6 (2002): 62-71.

Curran, Beverley and Mitoko Hirabayashi. "Translation: Making Space for a New Narrative in *Le désert mauve*." *International Journal of Canadian Studies/ Revue internationale d'études canadiennes*. 15 (1997): 109-20.

Daurio, Beverley. "Interview with Nicole Brossard." *Books in Canada*. XX.2 (1991).

Delepoulle, Anne-Marie. "La rage d'écrire, ou le défi féminin dans l'oeuvre de Nicole Brossard." Diss. Université de Paris-Val de Marne Paris XII, 1983.

Drapeau, Rose-Berthe. "Féminin singulier, pratique d'écriture, Brossard, Théoret." Diss. Université de Sherbrooke, 1985.

——. *Féminins singulier. Pratiques d'écriture; Brossard, Théoret*. Montréal: Triptyque, 1986.

Dumas, Ève. "Les voix lumineuses de la création." *La Presse* (14 août 2003). C3.

Dupré, Louise. "From Experimentation to Experience: Québécois Modernity in the Feminine." *A Mazing Space. Writing Canadian Women Writing*. Ed. Shirley Neuman and Smaro Kamboureli. Edmonton: Longspoon/ NeWest, 1986. 355-60.

——. *Les Stratégies Du Vertige. Trois Poètes: Nicole Brossard, Madeleine Gagnon, France Théoret*. Montréal: Les Éditions du Remue-Ménage, 1989.

——. "La critique au féminin: réalité et utopie." *Women's Writing and the Literary Institution/ L'Écriture au féminin et l'institution littéraire*. Claudine Potvin and Janice Williamson. Edmonton: Research Institute for Comparative Literature, University of Alberta, 1992. 69-76.

Durand, Marcella. "If I am really myself": On Translation (an Interview with Nicole Brossard)." *Verdure*. 5-6 (2002): 54-61.

Duranleau, Irène. "Le Texte moderne et Nicole Brossard." *Études littéraires*. 14.1 (1981) 105- 21.

Fiochetto, Rosanna. "Entrevue avec Nicole Brossard." *Tuttestorie*. 1 (1990).

Fisette, Jean. "Écrire pour le plaisir." *Voix et images du pays*. V.1 (1979): 197-201.

——. "L'Écrevisse et l'impossible: glose autour de deux textes de Nicole Brossard." *Voix et images*. XI (1985): 63-75.

Fisette, Jean and Michel van Schendel. "Entrevue avec Nicole Brossard." *Voix et Images du Pays*. III.1 (1977).

Fitzgerald, Judith. "Cutting to the Heart of the Matter." *The Globe and Mail*, "Books" (26 July 2003).

Flotow, Luise von. "Legacies of Quebec Women's 'Écriture au féminin': Bilingual Transformances, Translation Politicized, Subaltern Versions of the Text of the Street." *Revue d'études canadiennes/ Journal of Canadian Studies*. 30.4 (1995): 88-109.

Forsyth, Louise H. "The Novels of Nicole Brossard: an Active Voice." *Room of One's Own*. 4.1- 2 (1978): 30-38.

——. "L'écriture au féminin: *L'Euguélionne* de Louky Bersianik, *L'Absent aigu* de Geneviève Amyot, *L'Amèr* de Nicole Brossard." *Journal of Canadian Fiction*. 25-6 (1979): 199-211.

——. "The Radical Transformation of the Mother-Daughter Relationship in Some Women Writers of Québec." *International Journal of Canadian Studies/ Revue internationale d'études canadiennes*. 7.1 (1981): 44-50.

——. "Regards, reflets, reflux, réflexions — exploration de l'oeuvre de Nicole Brossard." *La Nouvelle Barre du Jour*. 118-9 (1982): 11-25.

——. "Les numéros spéciaux de *La (Nouvelle) Barre du Jour*. Lieux communs, lieux en recherche, lieu de rencontre." *Féminité, Subversion, Écriture*. Ed. Suzanne Lamy and Irène Pagès. Montréal: Éditions du Remue-Ménage, 1983. 175-84.

——. "Feminist Criticism As Creative Process." *In the Feminine. Women and Words/ Les Femmes et les mots*. Ann Dybikowski, Victoria Freeman, Daphne Marlatt, Barbara Pulling, and Betsy Warland. Edmonton: Longspoon Press, 1985. 87-94.

——. "Beyond the Myths and Fictions of Traditionalism and Nationalism: the Political in the Work of Nicole Brossard." *Traditionalism, Nationalism, and Feminism. Women Writers of Quebec*. Ed. Paula Gilbert Lewis. Westport & London: Greenwood Press, 1985. 157-72.

——. "Destructuring Formal Space/ Accelerating Motion in the Work of Nicole Brossard." *A Mazing Space. Writing Canadian Women Writing*. Ed. Shirley Neuman and Smaro Kamboureli. Edmonton: Longspoon/NeWest, 1986. 334-44.

——. "Nicole Brossard and the Emergence of Feminist Literary Theory in Quebec Since 1970." *Gynocritics/La gynocritique. Feminist Approaches to Writing by Canadian and Québécoises Women/ Approches féministes à l'écriture des Canadiennes et Québécoises*. Ed. Barbara Godard. Toronto: ECW Press, 1987. 211-21.

——. "Errant and Air-Born in the City." Nicole Brossard. *The Aerial Letter*. Trans. Marlene Wildeman. Toronto: The Women's Press, 1988. 9-26.

——. "Préface." Nicole Brossard. *Picture Theory*. 2 ed. Montréal: L'Hexagone, 1989. 7-26.

——. "Fernand Ouellette et Nicole Brossard — la poésie à caractère spéculaire: deux moments, deux écritures." *La Poésie de l'Hexagone*. Ed. Cécile Cloutier and Ben Shek. Montréal: L'Hexagone, 1990. 223-32.

——. "Les jeux de la représentation dans *Picture Theory* de Nicole Brossard." *Mises en scène d'écrivains. Assia Djebar, Nicole Brossard, Madeleine Gagnon, France Théoret*. Mireille Calle. Sainte-Foy: Les Éditions Le Griffon d'argile, 1993. 73-86.

——. "La critique féministe au Québec: une démarche créatrice." *L'autre lecture. La critique au féminin et les textes québécois*. Ed. Lori Saint-Martin. Montréal: XYZ Éditeur, 1994. 51-58.

——. "Bursting Boundaries in the Vast Complication of Beauty: Transported by Nicole Brossard's *Au présent des veines*." *Verdure*. 5-6 (2002): 100-08.

Fortier, France. "Entrevue avec Nicole Brossard." *Nuit Blanche*. 46 (1991).

——. "Entrevue avec Nicole Brossard." *Nuit Blanche*. 69 (1997): 84-87.

Gaudet, Gérald. "Entrevue avec Nicole Brossard." *Voix d'écrivains*. Montréal: Québec-Amérique, 1985. 215-25.

——. "Entrevue avec Nicole Brossard." *Lettres Québécoises*. 57 (1990).

Godard, Barbara. "*La Barre Du Jour*: vers une poétique féministe." *Féminité, Subversion, Écriture*. Ed. Suzanne Lamy and Irène Pagès. Montréal: Éditions du Remue-Ménage, 1983. 195- 205.

——. "*L'Amèr or the Exploding Chapter*: Nicole Brossard at the Site of Feminist Deconstruction." *Atlantis*. 9.2 (1984): 23-34.

——. "Mapmaking: A Survey of Feminist Criticism." *Gynocritics/ La gynocritique. Feminist Approaches to Writing by Canadian and Québécoises Women/ Approches féministes à l'écriture des Canadiennes et Québécoises*. Ed. Barbara Godard. Toronto: ECW Press, 1987. 1-30.

——. "Preface." Nicole Brossard. *Picture Theory*. Montréal: Guernica, 1991. 7-11.

——. "Producing Visibility for Lesbians: Nicole Brossard's Quantum Physics." *English Studies in Canada*. 21.1 (1995): 125-37.

——. "Theorizing Feminist Discourse/ Translation." *Translation, History, and Culture*. Eds. Susan Bassnett and André Lefevre. London: Cassell, 1990. 87-96.

——. "The Translator's Diary." *Culture in Transit: Translation and the Changing Identities of Quebec Literature*. Ed. Sherry Simon. Montreal: Vehicle Press, 1995.

Godard, Barbara, Daphne Marlatt, Kathy Mezei and Gail Scott. "Theorizing Fiction Theory." *Collaboration in the Feminine. Writings on Women and Culture from Tessera*. Toronto: Second Story Press, 1994. 53-62.

Gonnard, Catherine. "Entrevue avec Nicole Brossard." *Lesbia*. 120 (1993): 31-33.

Gould, Karen. *Writing in the Feminine. Feminism and Experimental Writing in Quebec*. Carbondale & Edwardsville: Southern Illinois University Press, 1990.

——. "Féminisme, postmodernité, esthétique de lecture: *Le désert mauve* de Nicole Brossard." *Le roman québécois depuis 1960: méthodes et analyses*. Ed. Louise Milot and Joop Lintrelt. Sainte-Foy: Presses de l'Université Laval, 1992. 195-213.

——. "Theory's Space in Recent Texts by Nicole Brossard and France Théoret." *Les discours féminin dans la littérature postmoderne au Québec*. Ed. Raija Koski, Kathleen Kells, and Louise Forsyth. San Francisco: Edwin Mellen Press, 1993. 127-41.

——. "Rewriting 'America': Violence, Postmodernity, and Parody in the Fiction of Madeleine Monette, Nicole Brossard, and Monique LaRue." *Postcolonial Subjects, Francophone Women Writers*. Ed. Mary Jean Green, Karen Gould, Micheline Rice-Maximin, Keith L. Walker, and Jack A. Yeager. Minneapolis: University of Minnesota Press, 1996. 186-209.

Guerreiro, Sandra. "'i write to make a presence in language'." *Verdure*. 5-6 (2002): 109-111.

Guillemette, Lucie. "Reduplication, traduction et palimpseste dans l'oeuvre de Nicole Brossard: l'inscription d'un espace féminin." *La Francophonie sans frontière. Une Nouvelle cartographie de l'imaginaire au féminin*. Ed. Lucie Lequin and Catherine Mavrikakis. Paris, Budapest & Torino: L'Harmattan, 2001. 181-95.

Havercroft, Barbara. "Hétérogénéité énonciative et renouvellement du genre: le *Journal intime* de Nicole Brossard." *Voix et images*. 64 (1996): 22-37.

Holbrook, Susan. "Delirium and Desire in Nicole Brossard's *Le désert mauve/Mauve Desert*." *Differences: A Journal of Feminist Cultural Studies*. 12 (2001): 70-85.

Huffer, Lynne. "Entrevue avec Nicole Brossard." *Yale French Studies*. 87 (1995): 115-21.

——. "From Lesbos to Montreal: Brossard's Urban Fictions." *Maternal Pasts, Feminist Futures*. Stanford: Stanford University Press, 1998. 117-33.

Joubert, Ingrid. "Entrevue avec Nicole Brossard." *Prairie Fire*. X.3 (1989).

Knutson, Susan et al. "Vers-ions Con-verse: A Sequence of Translations." *Tessera*. 6 (1989): 16-23.

——. "Nicole Brossard's Elegant International Play, in Canada." *Theoretical Discourse/ Discours théoriques*. Ed. Terry Goldie, Carmen Lambert, and Rowland Lorimer. 1994. 187-202.

——. "Reading Nicole Brossard." *Ellipse*. 53 (1995): 9-19.

——. *Narrative in the Feminine. Daphne Marlatt and Nicole Brossard.* Waterloo: Wilfrid Laurier University Press, 2000.

——. "Nouns, Pronouns, Verbs 'at eye level': Nicole Brossard's *Jeu de mots* & the Representation of Critical Subjectivity." *Verdure.* 56 (2002): 112-22.

Laliberté, Yves. "Deux recueils de poèmes où *Supprimer l'excentricité c'est s'abstenir*." *Incidences.* II-III.1 (1979): 77-97.

Lamoureux, Diane. *L'amère patrie. Féminisme et nationalisme dans le Québec contemporain.* Montréal: Les Éditions du Remue-Ménage, 2001.

Lamy, Suzanne. *d'elles.* Montréal: L'Hexaone, 1979.

——. *Quand je lis je m'invente.* Montréal: L'Hexagone, 1984.

——. "Les enfants uniques nés de père et de mère inconnus." *Gynocritics/La gynocritique. Feminist Approaches to Writing by Canadian and Québécoises Women/ Approches féministes à l'écriture des Canadiennes et Québécoises.* Ed. Barbara Godard. Toronto: ECW Press, 1987. 199-210.

Larson, Jacqueline and Jodey Castricano. "Blue Period – That's a Story: a Conversation with Nicole Brossard and Daphne Marlatt." *West Coast Line. A Journal of Contemporary Writing and Criticism.* 15 (1994-5): 29-53.

Leblanc, J. "Théorie et pratique de l'image photographique. De l'analogisme mimétique à la codification du «visuel-visible» (sur *Le désert mauve* de Nicole Brossard)." *Texte.* 21-22 (1997): 219-49.

Lévesque, Claude. "Le proche et le lointain." *Garder vive l'émotion.* Montréal: VLB Éditeur, 1994. 130-37.

Lotbinière-Harwood, Susanne de. *Re-Belle et infidèle/ The Body Bilingual.* Montréal: Les Éditions du Remue-Ménage; Toronto: Women's Press, 1991.

McPherson, Karen S. "Memory and Imagination in the Writings of Nicole Brossard." *International Journal of Canadian Studies/ Revue internationale d'études canadiennes.* 22 (2000): 87-102.

——. "Post(Modern) Script. D'une langue à l'autre or Speaking in Other Tongues: *Le désert mauve*." *Incriminations. Guilty Women/ Telling Stories.* Princeton: Princeton University Press, 1994.

Milot, Louise. "Margaret Atwood et Nicole Brossard: la question de la représentation." *Voix et images.* XI.1 (1985): 56-62.

——. "Nicole Brossard: une influence coûteuse." *Modernité/ Postmodernité du roman contemporain.* Ed. Jacques Allard and Madeleine Frédéric. Montréal: Les Cahiers du Département d'études littéraires, UQAM, 1987. 77-86.

Moisan, Clément. "Gwendolyn MacEwen – Nicole Brossard." *Poésie des frontières.* Montréal: Éditions HMH, 1979. 224-50.

Moyes, Lianne. "Composing in the Scent of Wood and Roses." *English Studies in Canada.* 21.2 (1995): 206-25.

——. "Caught in each other's dreams: Nicole Brossard's Portrait of Djuna Barnes." *Verdure.* 5-6 (2002): 91-99.

Nepveu, Pierre. "La Pensée/ L'impensable." *Lettres Québécoises.* 20 (1980): 24-25.

——. "Trois Romans de Nicole Brossard: une histoire au présent." *Incidences.* IV.2-3 (1980): 129-38.

——. *Écologie du réel*. Montréal: Boréal, 1988. 141-54.

Notar, Clea. "Interview with Nicole Brossard." *So to Speak*. Montréal: Vehicule Press, 1988. 123-143.

Parker, Alice A. "The Mauve Horizon of Nicole Brossard." *Quebec Studies*. 10 (1990): 107-119.

——. *Liminal Visions of Nicole Brossard*. New York: Peter Lang, 1998.

——. "Myth and Memory in Nicole Brossard's *Baroque d'aube* and *Vertige de l'avant-scène*." *Doing Gender. Franco-Canadian Women Writers of the 1990s*. Ed. Paula Ruth Gilbert and Roseanna Lewis Dufault. Madison & London: Teaneck Fairleigh Dickinson University Press & Associated University Presses, 2001. 36-52.

——. "Surviving in Another Tongue: Nicole Brossard's *Installations*." *Verdure*. 5-6 (2002):44-53.

Paterson, Janet M. *Moments postmodernes dans le roman québécois*. Ottawa: Presses de l'Université d'Ottawa, 1990. 109-23.

Paul, Catherine Anne. "Le processus de l'écriture d'un point de vue féministe: l'exemple de Nicole Brossard." Diss. Queen's University, 1984.

Perry, Catherine. "L'imagination créatrice dans *Le désert mauve*: transfiguration de la réalité dans le projet féministe." *Voix et images*. 57 (1994): 585-607.

Picard, Anne-Marie. "Arrêts sur images: identité et altérité dans *Le désert mauve* de Nicole Brossard et Rose Mélie Rose de Marie Redonnet." *Dalhousie French Studies*. 32 (1995).

Pouliot, Sophie. "La femme dans toute sa splendeur. Nicole Brossard, poète." *Le Devoir* (14 août 2003). (on dramatization of *Journal intime* directed by Brigitte Haentjens)

Prieto, René. "In-Fringe: The Role of French Criticism in the Fiction of Nicole Brossard and Severo Sarduy. *Do the Americas Have a Common Literature?* Ed. Gustavo Peres Firmat. Durham: Duke University Press, 1990. 266-81.

Rosenfeld, Marthe. "The Development of a Lesbian Sensibility in the Work of Jovette Marchessault and Nicole Brossard." *Traditionalism, Nationalism, and Feminism. Women Writers of Quebec*. Ed. Paula Gilbert Lewis. Westport & London: Greenwood Press, 1985. 227- 39.

Roy, André. "Entrevue avec Nicole Brossard." *Sortie*. 2 (1982).

Royer, Jean. "Entrevue avec Nicole Brossard." *Écrivains contemporains. Entretiens 2*. Montréal: L'Hexagone, 1985. 22-31.

——. "Entrevue avec Nicole Brossard." *Écrivains contemporains. Entretiens 3*. Montréal: L'Hexagone, 1985. 163-69.

Russo, Linda. "Sensational Intensities: Poetry and Prose: an Interview with Nicole Brossard." *Verdure*. 5-6 (2002): 123-37.

Saint-Martin, Lori. "Nicole Brossard et Daphne Marlatt: la fascination de l'écriture." *Les discours féminins dans la littérature postmoderne au Québec*. Ed. Raija Koski, Kathleen Kells, and Louise Forsyth. San Francisco: Edwin Mellen Press, 1993. 253-75.

Santa Cruz, Guadalupe. "Escritoras del Quebec: Las Coordenadas ebrias. Une lectura de Nicole Houde, Suzanne Jacob y Nicole Brossard." *Nomadías*. 7. Santiago,

Chile: CEGECAL (Centro de Estudios de Género y Cultura en América Latina, Facultad de Filosofía y Humanidades, Universidad de Chile). (forthcoming)

Santoro, Miléna. "Feminist Translation: Writing and Transmission Among Women in Nicole Brossard's *Le désert mauve* and Madeleine Gagnon's *Lueur*." *Women by Women. The Treatment of Female Characters by Women Writers of Fiction in Quebec since 1980*. Ed. Roseanna Lewis Dufault. Madison: Fairleigh Dickinson University Press; London: Associated University Presses, 1997. 147-68.

——. *Mothers of Invention. Feminist Authors and Experimental Fiction in France and Quebec*. Montreal and Kingston: McGill-Queen's University Press, 2002.

Saucier, Michèle. "L'oeil love volubilis. Les courbes d'une écriture. Lecture de/avec Nicole Brossard." Diss. Université de Sherbrooke, 1981.

Séguin, Lucie. "Femmage." *Les Cahiers de la Femme*. 1.3 (1979): 56-59.

Siemerling, Winfried. "The Visibility of the Utopian Form in the Work of Nicole Brossard." *Discoveries of the Other: Alterity in the Work of Leonard Cohen, Hubert Aquin, Michael Ondaatje, and Nicole Brossard*. Ed. Winfried Siemerling. Toronto: University of Toronto Press, 1994. 173-204.

Smart, Patricia. "Tout dépend de l'angle de vision." *Voix et images*. XI.2 (1985): 330-33.

Strachan, Fiona. "*Un livre* de Nicole Brossard, lecture fictive, lecture réelle." Diss. Université de Montréal, 1982.

Thompson, Dawn. "Re-Inventing the World: Calculating the Con/ Volutional Integrals of Holography in Nicole Brossard's *Picture Theory*." *Writing a Politics of Perception. Memory, Holography, and Women Writers in Canada*. Ed. Dawn Thompson. Toronto: University of Toronto Press, 2000. 16-42.

Vasseur, Annie Molin. "Entrevue avec Nicole Brossard." *Arcade*. 28 (1993).

Vidal, Jean-Pierre. "*French Kiss*." *Livres et auteurs québécois 1974*. Québec: Les Presses de l'Université Laval, 1975. 42-45.

Villemaire, Yolande. "Le French Kiss de la Vénus rouge." *Cul-Q*. 8-9 (1976): 63-85.

Wachtel, Eleanor. "Interview With Nicole Brossard." *Writers & Co*. Toronto: Alfred A. Knopf, 1996. 286-301.

Weir, Lorraine. "From Picture to Hologram: Nicole Brossard's Grammar of Utopia." *A Mazing Space. Writing Canadian Women Writing*. Ed. Shirley Neuman and Smaro Kamboureli. Edmonton: Longspoon/NeWest, 1986. 345-52.

Williamson, Janice. "Interview With Nicole Brossard." *Sounding Differences. Conversations with Seventeen Canadian Women Writers*. Ed. Janice Williamson. Toronto: University of Toronto Press, 1993. 57-74.

Biographical Notes on Contributors

Catharine Campbell was born and raised in the Eastern Townships of Québec. She recently completed her Ph.D. thesis in Comparative Canadian Literature at the Université de Sherbrooke, the title of which is "Hearing the Silence: A Legacy of Postmodernism." She teaches at the Writing Centre at Bishop's University and works part time at the local newspaper, *The Record*, works with her dogs and horses, and looks forward to an exciting academic career.

Katharine Conley is Professor of French at Dartmouth College. She has published essays on the work of Nicole Brossard, Francine Noel, and Anne Hébert. Her books include *Robert Desnos, Surrealism, and the Marvelous in Everyday Life* (U of Nebraska P, 2003) and *Automatic Woman: The Representation of Woman in Surrealism* (U of Nebraska P, 1996).

Louise Dupré, poet, novelist, essayist, critic and artist with more than a dozen titles to her credit, has published widely in Québec and elsewhere. Books of poetry: *La peau familière* (1983), *Chambres* (1986), *Bonheur* (1988), *Noir déjà* (1993), *Tout près* (1998), *Les mots secrets* (2002), *Sans témoin* (forthcoming). She published one of the first monographs on Brossard and *l'écriture au féminin* in Québec: *Stratégies du vertige. Trois poètes: Nicole Brossard, Madeleine Gagnon, France Théoret* (1989). Novels: *La memoria* (1996), *La Voie lactée* (2001), translated by Liedewij Hawke as *Memoria* (1999), *The Milky Way* (2002). She is Professor in the Département d'études littéraires de l'Université du Québec à Montréal and has been named a member of both the Académie des lettres du Québec and the Royal Society of Canada.

Louise Forsyth is Professor Emerita of Women's and Gender Studies, French and Drama at the University of Saskatchewan, where she was Dean of Graduate Studies and Research. Her publications include essays on Brossard, other Québec feminist writers, and feminist theatre in Québec and Canada. She was recently President of the Humanities and Social Sciences Federation of Canada.

Barbara Godard is Professor of English, Women's Studies and Social and Political Thought at York University. She has published many essays on Brossard, other Canadian and Québec writers, feminist literary theory, and translation theory. Her fourth translation of a Brossard text, *Journal intime*, has recently appeared. She edited an early collection of essays on *l'écriture au féminin: Gynocritics/ La gynocritique. Feminist Approaches to Writing by Canadian and Québécoises Women/ Approches féministes à l'écriture des Canadiennes et Québécoises*. She was founding co-Editor of *Tessera*, from which she edited *Collaboration in the Feminine: Writing on Women and Culture from* Tessera.

Susan Holbrook teaches North American literatures and Creative Writing at the University of Windsor. She is particularly interested in feminist experimental writing, publishing on Brossard and Gertrude Stein in such journals as *American Literature*, *differences* and *Tessera*. Her first book of poetry is entitled *misled* (Red Deer Press, 1999).

Lynette Hunter is Professor of the History of Rhetoric at the University of Leeds and Professor of Rhetoric at the University of California, Davis. She has written extensively on feminist writing and theory, and on Canadian literature and culture, in, for example, *Literary Value/ Cultural Power* (Manchester 2001). Her publications include *Outsider Notes. Feminist Approaches to Nation State Ideology, Writers/Readers and Publishing* (1996) and *Critiques of Knowing. Situated Textualities in Science, Computing and the Arts* (1999).Her current research is concerned with new democratic rhetorics and aesthetics.

Susan Knutson studied poetics at Selkirk College in British Columbia with Fred Wah. Her M.A. thesis (SFU) was a feminist study of William Morris's *Defence of Guenevere*, and her doctorate (UBC), under Lorraine Weir, was on Daphne Marlatt and Nicole Brossard. She has been teaching in the English Department at Université Sainte-Anne since 1988, where she now serves as Dean of Arts and Sciences. She has published numerous articles and a book, *Narrative in the Feminine: Daphne Marlatt and Nicole Brossard* (2001), and is the founding editor of *Port Acadie: Revue interdisciplinaire en études acadiennes/ An Interdisciplinary Review in Acadian Studies*.

Karen McPherson is Associate Professor of French and Francophone Studies at the University of Oregon. She is the author of *Incriminations: Guilty Women/Telling Stories* (Princeton UP 1994) and of the forthcoming *Archaeologies of an Uncertain Future: Recent Generations of Canadian Women Writing* (McGill-Queen's UP).

Alice Parker is Professor Emerita of French and Women's Studies at the University of Alabama. Her publications include a monograph, *Liminal Visions of Nicole Brossard* (1998), two volumes of feminist theory co-edited with Elizabeth Meese and numerous essays on French and Francophone women writers from the eighteenth century to the present.

Claudine Potvin was Chair, Women's Studies Program, University of Alberta and now teaches cultures and literatures from Quebec and Latin America in the Department of Modern Languages and Cultural Studies Her main fields of research are women's writing, gender theory, cultural studies, visual arts and literature. She has published a book on Medieval Castillian poetry, two collections of short stories (*Détails, Pornographies*), numerous articles in journals and books, and two edited collections of essays (*Women's Writings and the Literary Institution, Angéline de Montbrun*).